PREVENTIVE HOME MAINTENANCE

PREVENTIVE HOME MAINTENANCE

How to Detect and Prevent Structural, Electrical, Plumbing, and Other Problems in Your Home

THE AMERICAN SOCIETY OF
HOME INSPECTORS AND THE EDITORS OF
CONSUMER REPORTS BOOKS

Consumers Union
Mount Vernon, New York

LIBRARY OF CONGRESS CATALOGING-IN-PUBLICATION DATA

Preventive home maintenance: how to detect and prevent structural, electrical,
plumbing, and other problems in your home / The American Society of Home
Inspectors and the editors of Consumer Reports Books.
        p.   cm.—(The Homeowner's library)
        ISBN 0–89043–236–8
        ISBN 0–89043–390–9(HC)
  1. Dwellings—Maintenance and repair. 2. Dwellings—Inspection.
I. American Society of Home Inspectors. II. Consumer Reports Books.
    III. Consumers Union of the United States. IV. Series.
TH4817.P74   1990
643′.7—dc20   89–29637
                                               CIP

Design by Kathryn Parise
Illustrations by Laura Hartman Maestro

First printing, May 1990
Manufactured in the United States of America

Figure 2.4. on p. 26 reprinted by permission: American Institute of Architects, "Map of
Insulation Zones" and "Material Properties of Common Building Materials." In
Architectural Graphic Standards, 7th ed., ed. C. G. Ramsey and H. R. Sleeper, pp. 398–99.
John Wiley & Sons, Inc., New York, 1981.

Preventive Home Maintenance is a Consumer Reports book published by Consumers Union,
the nonprofit organization that publishes *Consumer Reports,* the monthly magazine of test
reports, product Ratings, and buying guidance. Established in 1936, Consumers Union
is chartered under the Not-For-Profit Corporation Law of the State of New York.

The purposes of Consumers Union, as stated in its charter, are to provide consumers
with information and counsel on consumer goods and services, to give information on
all matters relating to the expenditure of the family income, and to initiate and to
cooperate with individual and group efforts seeking to create and maintain decent living
standards.

Consumers Union derives its income solely from the sale of *Consumer Reports* and other
publications. In addition, expenses of occasional public service efforts may be met, in
part, by nonrestrictive, noncommercial contributions, grants, and fees. Consumers Union
accepts no advertising or product samples and is not beholden in any way to any
commercial interest. Its Ratings and reports are solely for the use of the readers of its
publications. Neither the Ratings nor the reports nor any Consumers Union publications,
including this book, may be used in advertising or for any commercial purpose.
Consumers Union will take all steps open to it to prevent such uses of its materials, its
name, or the name of *Consumer Reports.*

CONTENTS

CONTENTS

ACKNOWLEDGMENTS

Thanks to Ronald J. Passaro, who developed the idea for this book with the editors of Consumer Reports Books and served as the American Society of Home Inspectors' (ASHI) general editor and technical consultant. Thanks also to Vera Hollander Wadler for her coordinating and editing work for ASHI through numerous drafts of this manuscript. The comments, criticisms, and suggestions of ASHI's Technical Review Committee proved extremely valuable in writing and revising the manuscript. Thomas M. Byrne, R. A. Skip Campbell, John E. Cox, Robert G. Dunlop, Kurt F. Grashel, Stan Mitchell, and Robert T. Reeds were the committee members. Finally, ASHI's executive officers provided encouragement and support.

Special thanks to the following Consumers Union staff members and consultants for their review of portions of the final manuscript: Joe Csernica, Guy Henle, Dr. Malcolm Schoen, and Larry Seligson.

INTRODUCTION

"An ounce of prevention is worth a pound of cure." You are unlikely to find a subject where this homily holds more true than home maintenance and repair. A house represents a huge investment, and the costs of maintenance—protecting that investment—and repair when something goes wrong can be steep. Although maintaining the family car to reduce the likelihood of expensive repairs has become second nature for many of us, too few homeowners know about the simple inspections that can catch problems before they turn into major, costly repair jobs and the routine maintenance that can prolong the useful life of the parts and systems of a house. *Preventive Home Maintenance* provides you with this vital information in one concise reference; it is that indispensable owner's manual, which unfortunately did not come with your house.

Preventive Home Maintenance takes you system by system through the workings of a house teaching you how to spot the early signs and symptoms of trouble and explaining what maintenance needs to be done to keep a system running well. Since the key to proper maintenance and repair is understanding how things work and what causes them to break down, *Preventive Home Maintenance* first describes exactly how every system works. Each chapter then gives you simple inspection procedures that enable you to evaluate whether a struc-

ture is sound or a system is working properly. The book provides complete coverage, inside and out, from foundation to roof and basement to attic, including electrical, plumbing, heating, and air-conditioning systems. For the most part, you will need no more than your eyes, ears, and sense of touch, a pad and pencil to take notes, a flashlight to peer into dark spots, and an old screwdriver to use as a probe.

Preventive Home Maintenance also provides maintenance schedules designed to prevent problems from developing, and troubleshooting guidelines to help you track any symptom of trouble you find to its cause. It suggests the most effective remedies for the common problems that occur in houses, as well. Topics include wet basements, roof leaks, circuit shorts and overloads, window condensation, noisy plumbing, and weak or spotty heating.

Last but not least, *Preventive Home Maintenance* has a chapter on dealing with professionals, should it be necessary to use one. The chapter covers finding a reputable tradesperson or contractor, obtaining valid estimates, scheduling payments favorably to your interests, and putting language that protects you into a contract. These strategies are designed to increase the likelihood that the job is done to your satisfaction—the first time. In addition to many suggestions on how to avoid problems when working with tradespeople, the chapter also gives guidelines for resolving a dispute, if one arises.

How This Book Was Written

It is an age of specialization and there are experts in every field; house construction is no exception. But with all the different structures and systems that make up a house, few individuals have expertise in every area of house maintenance. Therefore, each chapter in *Preventive Home Maintenance* is written by a home inspector with special expertise in the subject it covers. The writers were drawn from the membership of the American Society of Home Inspectors (ASHI), which is a national, nonprofit organization that sets standards of practice and ethics for home inspectors. An ASHI technical review committee checked every chapter for thoroughness and accuracy. Consumers Union staff members and consultants reviewed the text further for accuracy, clarity, and usefulness.

As an organization, ASHI brings years of working knowledge of all facets of home construction to *Preventive Home Maintenance*. Many members are specialists in the fields of engineering, contracting, and architecture, all are professionals with far reaching experience. In their work, ASHI members must know intimately how things should be built, how they should work, and how they should stand the test of time. Here, members impart their accumulated knowledge to you so that you can best maintain and protect your home.

How to Use This Book

Home maintenance is a broad topic that requires you to become familiar with many different subjects. As with any large job, it's easier and less intimidating to break down "taking care of your home" into smaller tasks that are more easily accomplished. The work is also more likely to get done.

Each chapter gives an inspection, maintenance, and troubleshooting routine for a structure or system of a house. Thus, every chapter can be used

independently of the others, if necessary. Nevertheless, the many structures and systems of the house are inter-related, which is the reason the book is divided into two parts.

The first part deals mostly with the structural and weatherproofing components of a house: the foundation, roof, walls, and windows and doors. These structures and components work very much as a whole: for one to function properly, all must work well. The second part of the book covers the less visible systems: electricity, plumbing, heating, and air conditioning. Although these systems tend to be more discrete, they do relate to one another and to the other structures of the house.

When a subject concerns or interests you, you can turn to the relevant chapter and begin there. Obviously, start with "Roofs and Gutters" if you suspect the roof is leaking. You'll want to read first about the electrical system if none of the rooms in your house seem to have enough outlets. If you live in a very cold or warm climate, you may decide to begin with the chapters on heating or air conditioning.

We suggest, however, you read through the entire book to get a sense of how the house works as a whole. Moisture always finds its way to the attic; a leaky basement may cause condensation problems under the roof. The peeling ceiling that looks like a plumbing leak may be caused not by the water-supply system but by deteriorating grout around the base of the bathtub. A cold house in the winter may be caused by inadequate weatherproofing or a malfunctioning heating system, two very different problems.

Reading the book through will give you a sense of how each system of the house works synergistically with the others to keep you comfortable and safe. In addition, when you perform the individual inspections you will have a much better sense of where to look and what to look for with the knowledge you've gained about the whole house.

There is of necessity some overlap from chapter to chapter because the parts of a house do not stand alone. Roof maintenance and troubleshooting, for example, are covered in two separate chapters, "Attics" and "Roofs and Gutters," and the plumbing chapter is broken down into water supply, drainage, and venting sections. It's generally better, however, for you to focus on one inspection at a time, even if it means retracing your steps, rather than try to perform several different inspections simultaneously, which increases the likelihood that something important will be overlooked or forgotten.

Bear in mind that architectural styles and building practices vary. Not all of the systems and situations discussed will apply to your house. We have tried to address the styles, materials, and conditions that generally prevail, but a complete discussion of every possibility is beyond the scope of this—or any—book.

Set Realistic Goals

Sooner or later, we recommend you inspect your entire house by performing the inspections given chapter by chapter—but you don't have to do it all at once. Do a different inspection every other weekend, for example; spread the inspections out over an entire year. We often suggest repeating an inspection annually. As you learn what to look for, you can practice quick scans of the house as you go about your everyday living, looking for things that normally go unnoticed—a broken gutter, loose fixture, or damp patch in a corner. This kind of surveillance can nip problems in the bud. Those

people who develop confidence in their abilities may eventually want to combine inspections of two related systems, for example the foundation and exterior walls or windows and doors and interior floors, walls, and ceilings.

Follow at least one practical rule for maintenance: some maintenance is better than none. The chores that comprise routine maintenance can seem overwhelming, particularly when viewed as a whole. Breaking up those tasks seasonally will almost certainly guarantee that more maintenance is done.

We occasionally give recommendations about safety procedures or equipment you should use while inspecting or working. We urge you to follow those precautions.

Throughout the text we give suggestions about what you may want to do yourself and what work is best left to experts. Be realistic about the level of your skills and the time and effort you want to put into any project. Although *Preventive Home Maintenance* is not intended as an all inclusive fix-it manual, it does include step-by-step instructions for a few basic procedures, such as caulking, and will make you familiar with routine maintenance that should be done around the house. If you have the work done professionally, it will enable you to talk more knowledgeably and with greater confidence with the tradesperson about the job.

PART I

Around the House

1

FOUNDATION AND BASEMENT

The foundation of a building supports the structure above it and keeps the structure from shifting in any direction. Shifting produces cracks in the foundation itself as well as in the walls and ceilings of the house. It can cause stuck windows and doors, broken glass, other serious damage—even the total destruction of the dwelling.

A well-constructed and properly maintained foundation should last a lifetime. But a foundation that is built shoddily or built with materials that cannot endure the rigors of the local climate, or which is subjected to unusually severe conditions, is vulnerable to deterioration and ultimate failure. Subsequent damage to the dwelling above the foundation may vary from minor, easy-to-repair problems to major, hazardous structural damage, which is costly to correct.

Regardless of the age of your home, you should periodically examine the foundation from the inside and outside and look for signs of developing trouble. This is particularly important if you own a new house. An existing home may have had problems over the years that were corrected, but in a relatively short period, a new house will show signs of the wear and tear that result from poor construction or the local climate. Nevertheless, don't be lulled into a false sense of security because you own an older house with no apparent foundation problems. They may develop, for example, as a result of a bad winter, severe summer storms, or prolonged periods of rain. Before beginning your inspection, it's important that you know what type of foundation is used in your home—there are several varieties—and how the foundation is constructed.

Types of Foundations

Whatever material is used for the foundation, it should not only provide a rigid and stable base for the building but also keep the house dry and comfortable for the occupants. The material must resist decay by moisture and destruction by insects while in constant contact with the earth.

All types of foundations must meet the same building criteria. They must rest on solid ground. They must be built deep enough below the frost line so as not to be heaved and broken by the action of frost. (An exception is made in regions with permafrost, where buildings are constructed on top of the frozen ground, usually with insulation underneath to keep the frozen ground from thawing.) Foundations must also be provided with good drainage to prevent the buildup of hydrostatic pressure (the combined weight of water and wet soil) against the foundation. In addition, the soil around the foundation must be graded properly to ensure that rainwater and other runoff are continuously directed away from the foundation.

In locations with little or no frost, houses are often built on concrete slabs (see figure 1.1). Monolithic, or one-piece, slabs have thick edges around the perimeter and thickened areas under load-bearing walls. Other types of slabs feature support footings, which are made of poured concrete or

special concrete "footer" blocks set into the solid ground, on which the foundation walls rest. The slab can be poured within or on top of the walls. Some houses have reinforced concrete beams, called grade beams, that span two or more supporting walls at grade level.

Slab construction is also used in regions where the water table is high, since a basement and crawl space in such an area would often be flooded. The slab may be poured within, or sit on top of, a perimeter foundation wall.

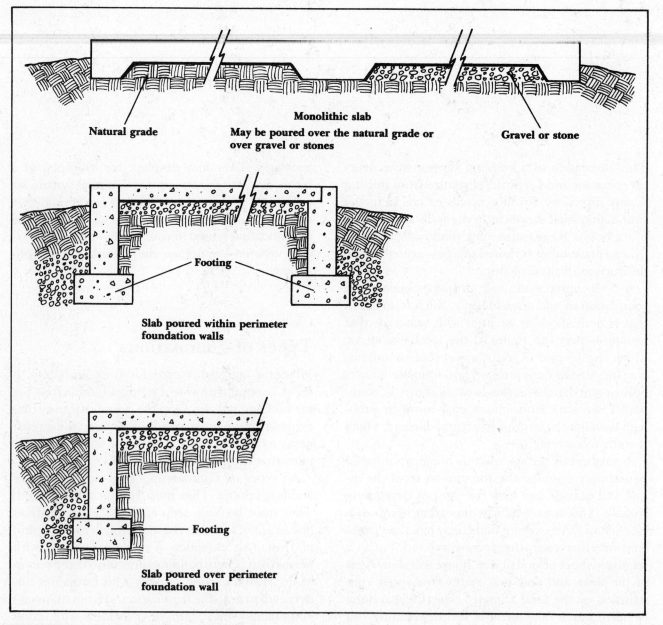

Natural grade

Monolithic slab
May be poured over the natural grade or over gravel or stones

Gravel or stone

Footing

Slab poured within perimeter foundation walls

Footing

Slab poured over perimeter foundation wall

FIGURE 1.1 Various slab constructions

At the seashore, where violent storms can cause flooding, or in areas where the weakness of the soil requires it, houses are often built on piers. These piers can be concrete or metal columns, bricks, blocks, wood posts, or pilings driven into the ground.

The majority of dwellings, however, are built on top of perimeter foundations that enclose either a crawl space or a full cellar or basement (see figure 1.2). In this classic foundation construction, concrete footings support foundation walls made of a variety of materials: poured concrete, concrete blocks, clay tiles, bricks, stones, granite slabs, or a mixture of the above. More recently, in some areas, foundation walls of pressure-treated wood resting on compacted crushed stone trenches have become popular. Basements usually have concrete slab floors; crawl spaces typically have dirt floors, since they remain unoccupied.

If your house was built in compliance with the local building code, chances are that the foundation was properly designed for the load-bearing capacity of the soil. Soils vary in their ability to support structures. A foundation's shape, design, and weight distribution—its "footprint," like that of a snowshoe—must match the bearing capacity of the soil on which it is built. But this is no guarantee against such problems as cracking from frost or hydrostatic pressure, leakage through a variety of

joints and cracks, or incursions from subterranean termites or other pests.

Cracks in the Foundation

Foundations crack for many reasons, and different foundation materials crack in different ways. Although most cracks are structurally insignificant, it takes a bit of detective work, and sometimes the help of an engineer or qualified inspector, to determine which cracks are important and which are not.

To begin your inspection, check the foundation on the outside; use a pad and pencil to take notes. As you walk around, look at its exposed surface carefully. If you find cracks, make a note of where they are located and how severe they appear. Later you'll want to look at them from inside the basement or crawl space to make a more complete determination about their seriousness.

Small hairline cracks are common and nothing to worry about; they may be due to shrinkage of the concrete or masonry and mortar joints as they cure and dry. (Hairline cracks may admit water if other conditions that encourage leaking are present.) Cracks wider than $\frac{1}{16}$ inch warrant further investigation—perhaps by a professional. Severe cracks in the foundation are caused by

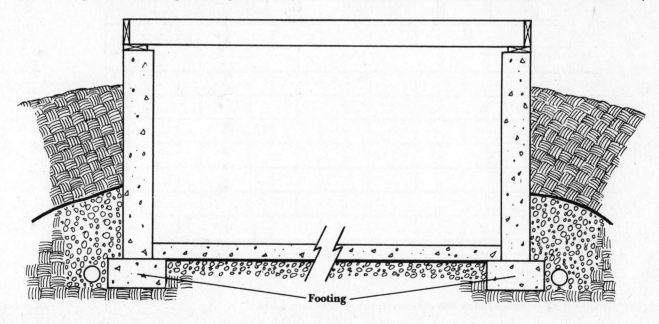

FIGURE 1.2 Perimeter foundation with slab poured as basement floor

heaving or settling of the soil or by lateral pressure against the foundation.

Heaving

In climates with long, cold winters, frost can penetrate below one or more sections of the footings, or even below the entire length of the foundation, causing the soil to expand, and "heave" or shift erratically as it freezes. This puts stress on the foundation walls.

In foundations built with individual masonry units such as blocks, stones, or bricks, cracks caused by heaving will generally have a step pattern that follows the mortar joints, although sometimes the masonry units themselves can crack. These cracks are therefore referred to as step, or ladder, cracks and may show some vertical displacement in which one face of the foundation wall has shifted upward, however slightly, in relation to the other (see figure 1.3).

In poured concrete foundations, cracks from heaving generally are vertical or near vertical and are often wider at the top than at the bottom, or vice versa. The cracks may occur anywhere in the wall but always at its weak points, usually near windows or other openings. They may also show vertical displacement.

With houses built on a monolithic slab, heaving may cause cracking of the slab, which may result in both horizontal and vertical separation, widening and unevenness, along the crack, as well as tilting or bulging of the affected sections.

In cold climates, an ice lens (a pocket of very wet soil that turns into a mass of ice) can also cause heaving of a section of wall or pier. As the soil expands, an ice lens can insinuate itself into a wall or pier and pull it apart or separate it from its footing. This is mainly a problem with masonry foundations other than poured concrete. Poured concrete piers are more likely to be lifted whole out of position, whereas poured concrete walls are

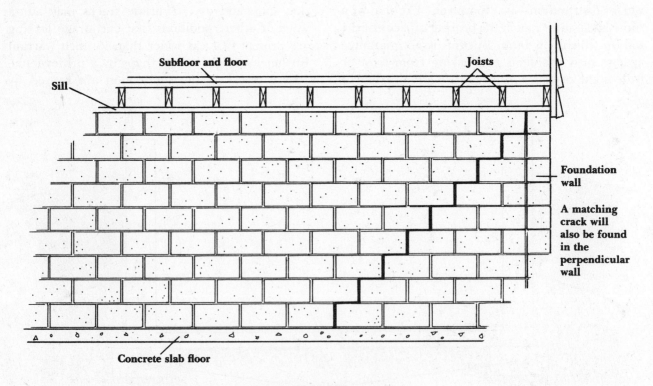

Cracks may run directly through masonry units.

FIGURE 1.3 A ladder crack

more likely to crack vertically, as discussed in the section on lateral pressure.

Some areas of the country have expansive clay soils, which increase in volume when they become saturated with water and decrease in volume when they become dry. The drastic changes in volume can cause serious heaving problems and structural damage. Expansive clays that become too wet can, in fact, expand so much that they implode the foundation. When a clay soil dries out, it can pull away from the foundation. To prevent this pushing and pulling, the moisture content of the expansive clay soils must be kept constant.

Generally, however, heaving can be prevented by keeping the soil under and around the foundation as dry as possible. This goal is usually realized if the land near the house has been graded correctly, the perimeter drains have been properly installed and work well, and coarse backfill that drains well has been used to fill in around the foundation.

Settling

Settling of the soil usually occurs when the foundation was not poured on solid ground or when the ground has shifted because of tremors caused by the use of heavy equipment, blasting nearby, an earthquake, or an underground watercourse. Settling may also result if the foundation footings do not match the load-bearing capacity of the soil on which they rest. Cracks caused by settling resemble those produced by heaving, so it may be difficult for you to distinguish between the two. If you are in doubt, call in a qualified professional to piece together the evidence and determine the cause of the cracking.

In older homes, cracks from settling may indicate a process completed long ago and may require no repair. With new buildings, or whenever settling has caused severe structural sagging or misalignment, it may be necessary to make major repairs after discussing the situation with a specialist. Given the high cost of major repairs on foundations, it may be a wise choice to call in an independent consultant who will reap no financial gain from any needed work (see chapter 11).

Lateral Pressure

Cracks in foundations can also be caused by heavy, wet soil pressing laterally against a foundation; by sideways pressure from frost or ice; by premature backfilling of the trench around the foundation (before the foundation has cured and been reinforced); or by heavy equipment coming too close to the foundation. Moreover, the excavation around the foundation must not be backfilled with large rocks or frozen chunks of earth because the resulting stress on the foundation may cause it to crack.

With masonry foundation walls, this pressure will usually show itself through one or more long horizontal cracks in the top half of the wall as seen from inside the basement or crawl space. After your tour of the outside perimeter, check along each interior wall from one end to the other, looking for both vertical and horizontal inward bowing or simply for jackknifing action at the point where the cracks are visible. There may also be lateral displacement; the upper portion of the wall above the crack may move inward and overhang the lower portion.

In poured concrete foundations, the cracks caused by lateral pressure are again generally vertical or near vertical, and occur more often near a break in the wall such as a window or other opening. Lateral pressure causes lateral displacement, so that on one side of the crack the wall may be pushed inward more than it is on the other side, but not vertical displacement, as with cracks caused by heaving or settling.

If your house has concrete piers that lack footings, or if the piers are not attached to the footings with steel pins, the piers may lean or even be lifted by pressure from frost. Such pressure can displace or shear off concrete piers that are reinforced with steel rods if the steel does not extend to the top of the piers. In either case, any beam that rested on the piers is now without support.

Condensation

Condensation is a very common occurrence that plagues masonry foundation walls in the humid summer months. The soil in contact with the foundation does not experience great temperature variations over the seasons, except near the surface. As a result, masonry walls remain cool through most of the warm weather. If hot, humid air enters the basement or crawl space, condensation occurs on the cool masonry surfaces. Condensation can be so extensive that it mimics a leak.

In hot, humid climates, condensation will also occur on the floor joists and subfloor exposed in crawl spaces and basements as warm, moist air penetrates and comes in contact with cooler surfaces. Although condensation does not damage concrete or masonry walls, it can cause wood joists and subflooring to rot and also attracts wood-destroying insects. It is therefore advisable to keep basement windows and crawl-space foundation vents closed in hot, humid weather. Ventilate basements and crawl spaces only on cool, dry days.

When you have the problem of a wet foundation, there may be a problem in the attic as well (see chapter 2). In the winter, as the moisture in a home spreads, it will condense on the roof structure. Home inspectors often find rotted roof sheathing in conjunction with wet foundations.

You may also notice whitish deposits on the surface of your foundation. Known as efflorescence, this is the result of moisture getting on the walls, dissolving salts contained within them, and then depositing the salts on the wall surface as the moisture evaporates. Efflorescence is not serious and doesn't cause damage to the walls by itself. To remove the deposits, use a stiff brush either dry or with a little bit of water.

Leaks in the Foundation

To check for leaks, you will have to go to the basement or enter the crawl space, if reasonable access is available, and make an inspection from inside the foundation. Unless there is plenty of light available, you'll need a strong flashlight. Wear old clothes or overalls in a crawl space.

Actual damp or wet areas are obvious, but even if you find the foundation dry, look for signs of past leakage or dampness such as water stains at the base of the staircase or on any wood in contact with the floor. Check for discoloration or stains on the walls or floor. Touch the stained areas to check

for dampness. If the concrete floor is tiled, look for whitish streaks in and around the tile joints and for cracked, brittle, or curling tiles.

There's a simple test to help you distinguish between a seepage through the walls and condensation from inside air. Smooth a 12-inch square of aluminum foil or plastic wrap against the wall and tape all four edges, making sure the bond is as airtight as possible. Leave it up a day or two. Then remove the foil or wrap. If the side that was next to the wall is wet, seepage is occurring. If the outside is wet, condensation is occurring. (*Note:* Both may be occurring.)

The single most common source of water that finds its way into the basement through the foundation is rain or melted snow, technically known as surface water. The most common *cause* of water entering the basement is faulty surface grading. When the land around a house is sloped toward the building, the force of gravity pulls the water down along the foundation wall and through cracks, openings, or weak joints. In light of this fact, it makes sense for you to take another walk around the outside of your house and conduct a thorough investigation of the conditions that may be responsible for the water leakage. Look for any of the following:

- A negative grade, which is ground that slopes toward the house from one or more directions.
- Depressions around the foundation that can collect water.
- Stoops, driveways, walks, or patios sloping toward the house. If necessary, use a level to determine the direction of slope.
- A clogged drain at the base of stairs from the basement to the outside. A drain clogged with matted leaves may cause water to form a pond or the dry well beneath the drain may be silted up. Check the drain by running water from a garden hose for 2 or 3 minutes to see if it backs up.
- Leaky or clogged gutters and downspouts (see chapter 3). Check from a ladder, and run water from a garden hose through them after removing all debris.
- A disconnected downspout shoe, which is the curved piece at the base of the downspout.
- A missing or improperly placed splash block, which is the flat pan that should direct down-

spout water away from the foundation (see chapter 3).

- A clogged or broken underground drainpipe built into a patio or paved area, or underneath a downspout. Run a garden hose into the drainpipe for several minutes, and look for water gurgling at the surface or leaking into the basement or crawl space.
- A rotting tree stump near the foundation.
- Window wells filled with wet leaves or standing water.

Leaks are most likely to occur during or shortly after prolonged or heavy rainstorms. Water may seep down as far as the footings and through the joints of the foundation walls and floor into the basement or crawl space.

If, on the other hand, leaks occur several days after rainy weather, or during spring thaw in regions where the snowcover is substantial, they may be due to a rising water table. (The water table is the level of underground water; it fluctuates according to the amount of rainfall or melting snow.) Another underground source of water, particularly in mountainous areas, may be a sub-surface spring or a waterway that follows a rock ledge.

Sump Pumps

Check that your sump pump, if you have one, is not discharging water into the septic system and that it is connected to the storm sewage system, *not* to the sanitary sewage system, unless permitted by your local building code. (Some communities allow both systems; check with your local officials.) The pump should not discharge water into a dry well either, because dry wells may silt up over time and then will usually fail when they are needed most—in periods of heavy or prolonged rain.

Finally, the pump should not discharge immediately outside the foundation walls; this would allow water to run back down along the walls to the sump. It should discharge onto a concrete splash block tilted away from the house or into a drainage pipe that carries the water away from the foundation.

Exterior Drainage and Grading

The most effective means of controlling water leaks from sub-surface water is a system of properly built foundation drains, which are also called perimeter drains and footing drains. Installed during the construction of a house, foundation drains are designed to dispose of excess water primarily from rising water tables and underground waterways. But if the drain is improperly installed or if it deteriorates, it may be the cause of foundation leakage.

Where the lay of the land permits it, a foundation drain system generally "daylights," or discharges, in the open. You can tell whether the system is working by looking for discharge in periods of heavy rains or when snowcover melts. On flat terrain the drain may discharge into an underground dry well, or it may be connected to a sump inside the basement or crawl space. If the drain or the dry well silts up, or if the outlet of the pipe becomes blocked by soil, vegetation, or an animal's nest, the drain will no longer function and leaks may occur.

To build a house, a hole larger than the foundation is dug so that workers can have access to both sides of the foundation wall. Once a perimeter drain has been installed around the foundation footing, the trench between the unexcavated earth and the foundation is backfilled, first with stone or gravel and then with some of the excavated soil (see figure 1.4). Even if the builder correctly sloped the ground away from the foundation during the final grading, the backfill is looser than the undisturbed soil. In time, gravity with the help of rainfall will compact the backfill, which creates a moatlike depression around the foundation.

Rainwater is trapped in the depression and runs down along the foundation until it reaches the drains around the footings and the undisturbed soil. If there is no functioning drain, a wall of water builds up hydrostatic pressure and leaks occur through any weak part of the foundation. Flower beds adjacent to the foundation wall contribute to this problem (see figure 1.5). Heavy mulching worsens it by preventing the soil from drying out between wettings. These and other depressions can all be easily seen with the naked eye, but if in doubt use a level to check the grade for proper pitch, or run water to see in which direction it flows.

Stoops, walks, patios, open porches, and drive-

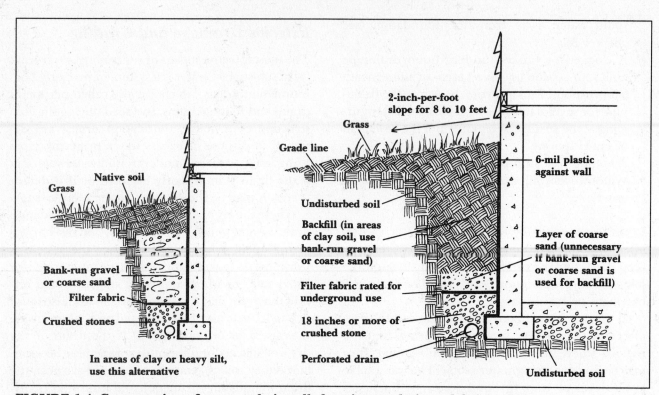

FIGURE 1.4 Cross section of a correctly installed perimeter drain and finish grade

ways, even if properly built to shed water away from the foundation, very often are affected by settling backfill. These structures can break off near or at the point where undisturbed earth and backfill meet. The section bridging the backfill trench begins to tilt toward the house, directing water toward the foundation wall itself (see figure 1.6).

Although foundation leakage caused by any of the above problems can occur in any soil, it is far less likely to occur in coarse, gravelly soils where drainage below the foundation is good. But most houses are built on and backfilled with expansive soils, such as clays and silts. Drainage (percolation) through these soils is very slow and difficult. In many areas of the United States, notably the Gulf and Atlantic Coast states and parts of the Midwest, expansive soils may compound leakage problems.

When the grading around a foundation is properly sloping away from it, these expansive soils prevent quick percolation and allow fast runoff. But any negative grading or depression collects water near or against the foundation where these soils can absorb more and more water and hold it for extended periods. The heavy soil can become unstable, applying substantial pressure against the foundation walls. In cold climates, frost causes these soils to expand considerably, and the foundation may crack under the pressure. In extreme cases, particularly with houses built on slopes, heavy, unstable soil can lead to landslides. For more information on the type of soil conditions in your area, contact your area's U.S. Department of Agriculture Cooperative Extension Service.

Insects

Insects are another potential problem to consider when examining a foundation. The most common are subterranean termites. These are worms, not ants. The workers and soldiers are small, wingless insects, creamy in color, with only two parts to their bodies, a head and a larger abdominal section. Unlike wingless workers and soldiers, breeding termites are dark, flying insects with two pairs of milky wings of the same size and straight antennae.

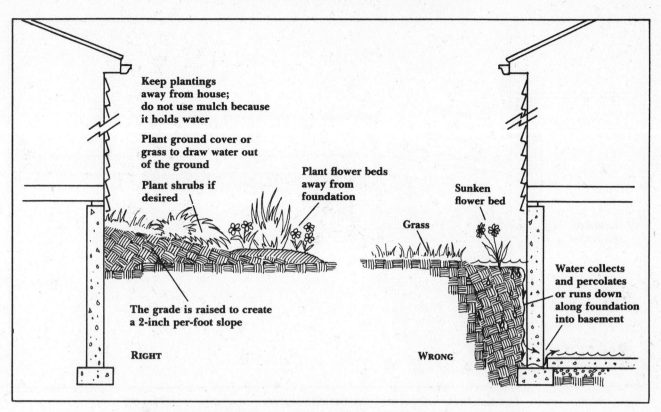

Keep plantings away from house; do not use mulch because it holds water

Plant ground cover or grass to draw water out of the ground

Plant shrubs if desired

Plant flower beds away from foundation

Sunken flower bed

Grass

The grade is raised to create a 2-inch per-foot slope

RIGHT

WRONG

Water collects and percolates or runs down along foundation into basement

The cross section shows common problems (*right*) and the correct way to prevent them (*left*).

FIGURE 1.5 Right and wrong grading and flower bed

Breeding termites also have two parts to their bodies. In contrast, carpenter ants have three parts to their bodies, two pairs of transparent wings of *different* size, and *bent* antennae.

Termite grubs live in colonies below ground and cannot survive exposure to air and light. To reach the food supply that the wood and other cellulose materials in a house provide, they build earth tunnels the size of knitting needles along the foundation walls to get to their feasting channels in the framing of the house. These earth tunnels are not always visible from either the outside or the inside surfaces of the foundation walls, or the surfaces of supporting piers, because termites try to build tunnels within the voids and cracks of these structural elements. Nevertheless, you should thoroughly examine all exposed foundation and pier surfaces for tunnels every year.

There are three other kinds of termites that are not as widespread as the subterranean termites, infesting mostly the Southern states: dry wood ter-

mites, damp wood termites, and Formosan termites. They do not need contact with the ground and often attack wood in attics. They are not easy to recognize. If you live in an area they are known to inhabit, call a licensed pest control firm to check the house out and recommend treatment if necessary.

Incursions by other insects, such as sow bugs, millipedes, centipedes, earwigs, silver fish, and spiders are not serious in themselves, but they indicate a humid environment, and the increased potential for rot and decay. If the infestation is severe, investigate the cause with the help of experts. You can call a pest control firm or take a sample of the insect to your local Cooperative Extension Service for identification and advice on control.

Carpenter ants are another bane of the homeowner. They do not feed on the wood in the house; they simply excavate damp or rotting wood to build nests and in some regions also attack the adjacent

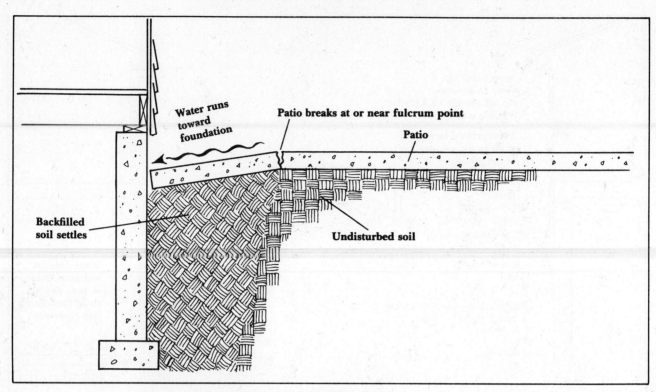

The slab broke off because the backfill settled.

FIGURE 1.6 Broken patio slab directing water toward basement

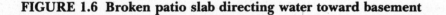

dry wood. Their presence in large numbers can almost be considered a blessing in disguise; they pinpoint areas of long-term water damage so you can take corrective measures.

Treatment for the prevention or eradication of termites or carpenter ants is not a do-it-yourself project. It is a highly specialized task that belongs in the hands of properly trained professionals. It requires a thorough knowledge of where to look and what to look for and what actions to take.

Radon

The gas radon is a product of the decomposition of underground radioactive elements that escapes into the environment from the earth. Sometimes radon leaks into basement and crawl-space walls through cracks and other openings. Much publicity has been given to this cancer-producing contaminant in recent years as our knowledge about it has increased.

All houses should be screened for radon, particularly those in areas of suspected contamination. You can hire a reputable and experienced testing company to come and set detectors and retrieve them some time later for analysis. Or you can get detectors yourself, set them up as instructed, and send them to a reliable laboratory for testing—at much less cost. The most practical approach for most people is to use two charcoal-absorbent detectors—one in the basement and one in the living room—under conditions when the windows are generally closed, in the fall-to-spring period. This will provide the lowest-cost tests and the most rapid, reasonably reliable results.

You can get more information from your local or state health department, including advice on how to mitigate the intrusion of this odorless and colorless gas into your basement and house. Sealing all cracks is a good way to start. But refer to reliable literature to lead you through the detection process and the corrective steps best suited to your area.

A quick check for radon taken in a few minutes on any given day is of little use except to tell you what the radon level is at the time of the test. The level of contamination varies constantly and is affected by many factors. At this time the recognized procedure encompasses a minimum testing period of several days, and preferably weeks or months.

Controlling Leaks

Having thoroughly inspected your foundation from the inside and outside, and having determined that a leak, not simple condensation, is the source of your water problems, there are a variety of remedies available depending on the type of problem and its seriousness. The measures listed here involve some effort and expense, and you should consider carefully whether or not they are for you or a professional contractor to undertake.

If the scope of the work involved is more than you can handle yourself, use the knowledge acquired in reading this chapter to help you determine whether the contractor is trying to sell you a much bigger job than you really need. If you intend to have the work done by a professional, read Chapter 11.

The majority of leakage problems can be solved by directing surface water away from the building, for example, by regrading around the foundation or installing splash blocks under downspouts. Yet some specialists will try to sell you high-ticket solutions far beyond what's required. Get several opinions and proposals for solutions from general contractors familiar with the problem so that you can make an informed decision.

Regrade the Surface

If you find negative grade, sunken areas, or depressions around and near the foundation, correct them by raising the grade with topsoil or loam with some clay content. Do not use sand or gravelly, coarse soil, because the objective is to drain water *away* from the foundation, not down *through* the added soil.

You should aim for a slope of 1 to 2 inches per horizontal foot and continue the slope as far as

possible from the foundation. It is best to start near the foundation with a full 2-inch-per-foot slope and then gradually lessen it as you reach 4 to 6 feet from the foundation. Keep in mind that most building codes require a clearance of 6 to 8 inches between the soil and the bottom of the siding of the house.

Build Up Window Wells

You may need to extend the height of basement window wells to be able to raise the dirt level of basement or crawl-space windows or vents. The floor of the well should remain at least 6 inches and preferably 12 inches below the windowsills, so do not remove the existing wells; extend them instead. Use prefabricated window-well extensions or make your own, as needed, with bricks, flagstones, or pressure-treated lumber.

You can make window-well extensions out of bricks by digging a trench 4 inches deep around the outside perimeter of existing window wells. Set the bricks upright in this trench with their 4-inch width against the well rim. Backfill the trench and tamp it down. This will raise the top of the well 4 inches above the rim since bricks are 8 inches long.

If you need to raise the grade more than 4 inches, use the narrowest flagstones you can buy or have them cut in 6- or 8-inch widths; their length should be twice the height of the extension you need. Follow the same procedure as for installing bricks. In making extensions from pressure-treated lumber, you can use ready-made 4-by-4 timber or a plank 2 inches by whatever depth you need to raise the grade.

Relocate Flower Beds

Instead of planting flower beds against the foundation, consider either grass or a thick ground cover with a heavy root system, such as pachysandra, hosta, sedum, or whatever species thrives in your area. Shrubs are fine, but don't plant them too close to the foundation; give them room to grow without coming into contact with the house walls.

Flower beds can be just as attractive if they are placed a few feet away from the house (you'll have the added advantage of seeing them from the inside as well). They will also get the run-off water from the slope above and will be easier to tend because you'll have access from two sides. If you make a masonry walkway between the foundation and flower bed, out of brick or flagstone, for example, make certain it slopes away from the house and does not dam up the run-off.

Fill in Depressions

If you find that runoff has eroded channels that allow water to run along the foundation and under masonry stoops, patios, walks, or porches, fill the channels with as impervious a soil mixture as you can find. Pack it down as much as possible so all voids are filled completely; then tamp and slope the soil next to the structure so that water runs away from the foundation.

Correct the Slope of Concrete Structures

If you find a masonry stoop, patio, porch, or walk sloping toward the house, there may be no need to remove it, even if it is cracked. It is often possible to cover the structure with a new layer of mesh-reinforced concrete, tapered to reverse the slope, or with bricks or flagstones set higher at the foundation than at the side away from it. Be sure the new construction is properly flashed where it meets the house, to protect any wood from water damage. (Flashing is made of one or more metal pieces that prevent water from penetrating at joints between various materials.)

Driveways that direct water against the house are somewhat harder to handle. It may be possible to add a layer of concrete or asphalt mix over the section against the foundation to direct the water away, but traffic, running water, and frost can affect the longevity of the repair. You may have to settle for an asphalt or concrete curb built against the foundation to protect its joint with the drive-way. At worst, the offending section may have to be removed and relaid to slope away from the foundation.

Generally, any of this major masonry work is best left to a competent general or masonry contractor.

Maintain Gutters and Downspouts

Gutters and downspouts direct thousands of gallons of water away from your foundation each year. Therefore, you should maintain them and keep them in good working order (see chapter 3).

In areas where gutters and downspouts are not practical and seldom used, such as the cold regions of the North, water falling off the roof must be controlled to prevent it from eroding the soil, creating its own trench, and getting trapped against the house. The best method is to lay rectangular flagstones (1 inch thick by 12 inches wide) end to end, flush with the grade, and underneath the drip line of the roof. This narrow strip of durable stones, when laid on ground sloping *away* from the foundation, not only will control splashing against the building but also will direct water away from it.

Create a Swale to Redirect Water

When a house sits so low to the ground on a flat lot that it is impossible to raise the grade against the foundation, the alternative is to lower the grade in a ring several feet away from the house, thereby creating a gently sloping swale (see figure 1.7). A swale leads water to a lower area, or it will simply hold the water in a shallow, moatlike ring around, yet away from, the house, where slow percolation and evaporation eventually dispose of it.

The job of creating a swale is probably best handled by a contractor. If it is impossible to bring machinery to the location because of trees, plantings, or other obstructions, the alterations to the grade will have to be performed by hand, by a contractor or the homeowner.

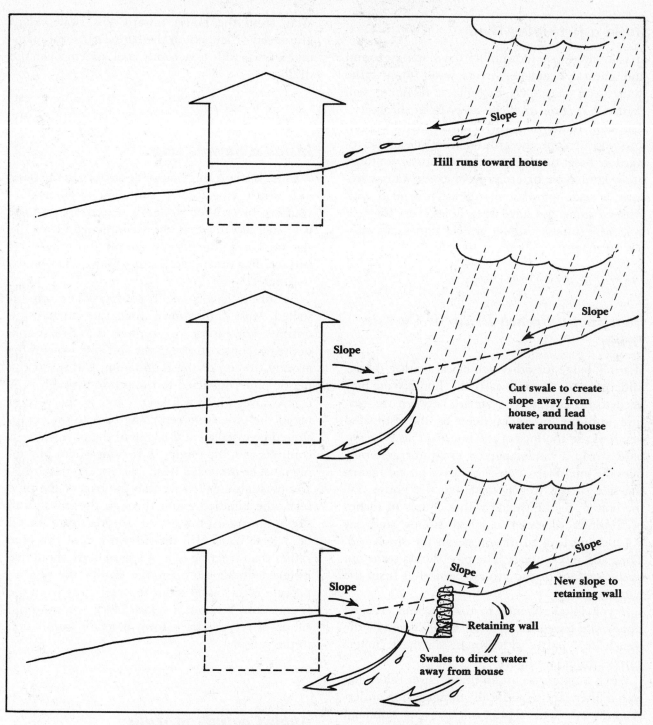

Slope

Hill runs toward house

Slope

Slope

Cut swale to create slope away from house, and lead water around house

Slope

Slope

New slope to retaining wall

Slope

Retaining wall

Swales to direct water away from house

A retaining wall can be built in two or more stages to create a stepped landscape and planting areas.

FIGURE 1.7 A swale or retaining wall directing water away from house

Build a Retaining Wall

If your house sits downhill from sloping ground and natural drainage directs water toward the house, you may have to build a retaining wall (figure 1.7) some distance away from the house. The wall should be constructed so that it also allows you to slope the ground from the house toward its base, thus reversing the natural contours of the land. Note that to prevent excess water pressure, a retaining wall should be backfilled with crushed stone and have weep holes every few feet at its base (unless it's built of field stones laid without mortar).

Construct a French Drain or Curtain Drain

If a hill, ledge, or other geological feature directs underground water toward the house, you may need to dig a trench in an arc between the feature and the house as deep as the estimated depth of the footings of the house. (This is heavy, hard work; a landscaper or excavator generally does the job.) Place a piece of heavy plastic against the side of the trench closest to the house. Fill the bottom of the trench with a couple of inches of 1½-inch diameter crushed stones, and lay a 4-inch perforated drainpipe on the stone bed. Then add more stones. The pipe should come out to the surface of the ground, downhill from the house.

If you fill the trench to the top with crushed stones, you have built a French drain; if you fill the trench only partly with stones, you have built a curtain drain (see figure 1.8).

When building a curtain drain, cover the stones with a filter fabric specifically designed for underground use. The fabric will prevent sediment from blocking the drainage while still permitting penetration of water. A layer of coarse sand or other coarse material should be placed on top of the filter fabric to keep it from clogging. Complete the backfill with the native soil removed from the trench, but shape the ground on each side of the trench so that it slopes toward it in a swale fashion. The grade should always slope away from the house toward this swale. Plant grass seed or lay sod on the bare earth, and maintain a lawn with a vigorous root system over the drain.

Install a Sump Pump

A sump is a hole dug below the surface of the floor into which a perforated container or liner, surrounded by crushed stones, is placed. Its purpose is to collect water that has accumulated below the slab or that is drained into the sump off the slab's surface. The function of a sump pump is to remove that water.

Be sure to have a quality submersible pump installed. Most pumps must discharge water to the outside. The easiest way to do so is to drill a hole of the proper size through the rim joist, which runs around the top of the foundation, and insert the plastic pipe connected to the pump through it. A check valve, which will keep water in the vertical leg of the pipe from returning back to the sump, should be installed at the base of the pipe where it connects with the pump. In regions where plumbing must be protected from freezing temperatures, you must also make sure that the part of the pipe *inside* the building going through the house wall slopes downward toward the outside for at least 2 or 3 feet. Water will then drain out of the pipe rather than freezing in it. A splash block should be installed under the discharge end of the pipe to prevent erosion and to move water away from the foundation. Without a splash block, water would simply be recycled back down along the foundation to the sump.

Apply Coatings to Walls

Although there are a number of wall coatings available that are effective in curing basement leaks from the inside, they should be used *only* in very minor cases of leakage. Although it is effective, it does permit the water to build up inside hollow masonry units and to saturate the soil outside. This greatly increases fluid pressure against the foun-

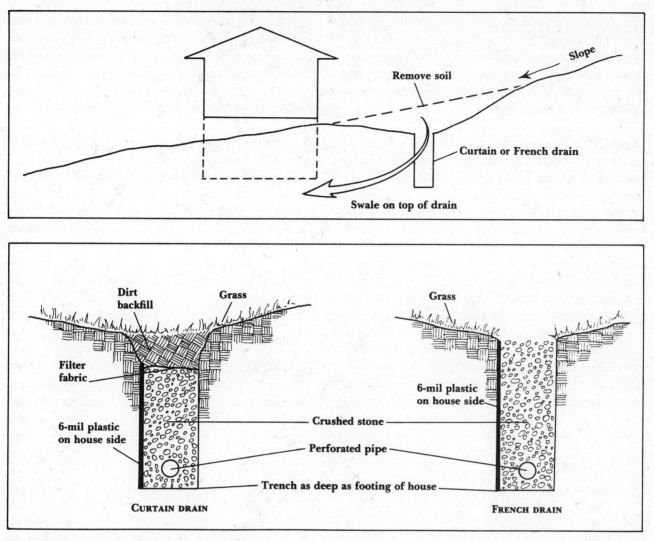

FIGURE 1.8 Curtain and French drains

dation and increases the level of moisture that evaporates into the house. The end result may be damaged walls and sudden flooding of the basement. At the very least, the great increase in moisture within the house can lead to sticking windows and doors, mold and mildew, condensation on glass, and rotting of the roof and other wooden structures. Where leakage is serious, a coating applied to the inside walls of a foundation will probably fail eventually.

Unfortunately, builders frequently fail to properly apply the various coatings or other systems that are meant to be used on the *outside* of foundation walls. Therefore, they tend to fail over time, and reapplication is expensive because the foundation must be excavated.

Other Measures

When serious leakage cannot be controlled by any of the means described above, there are three possible solutions, each of which requires the services of a competent and experienced contractor.

You may wish to install hollow, glass-fiber baseboards inside the foundation. These devices create a collection gutter at the base of the walls (through holes drilled in the foundation) and direct water to a sump pump.

As another solution, you can install a subslab interior drain. This involves breaking up and removing a strip of the concrete slab from around the base of the interior foundation walls, removing the gravel and soil down to the base of the footing, and installing a perforated drainpipe in a crushed-stone bed leading to a sump equipped with a submersible pump (see figure 1.9). Small holes are drilled at the base of the foundation wall to permit water passage to the pipe drain. New concrete is poured to repair the floor.

Alternatively, you can rebuild the foundation drains. This is the best, but also the most expensive, solution. A contractor excavates outside along the foundation to the bottom of the footings. Heavy plastic, such as 6-mil polyethylene, is applied against the foundation walls and overlaps the footings as a water repellent. Seams should be avoided as much as possible by using full-length rolls. It is unnecessary to clean and coat the walls with commercial waterproofing materials.

A thin layer of crushed stones having a 1½-inch diameter should then be laid in the trench, followed by a 4-inch, perforated drainpipe with the holes facing down. More crushed stones should be carefully placed over and around the pipe to a total depth of at least 12 to 18 inches. The stones should be covered with an underground-type filter fabric, which in turn should be covered with a layer of porous material such as coarse sand or bank gravel.

In areas of heavy silt or clay, it is advisable to fill the bulk of the excavation with this coarse material and to use the heavy soil only at the top, sloping away from the foundation to reduce percolation to a minimum and to permit vegetation to grow. This is particularly important in cold regions where deep frosts are common.

The perforated drainpipe should be connected to a solid pipe that reaches daylight downhill from the house, if feasible, or it should go under the house footing and terminate in a sump equipped with a submersible pump.

Crawl Spaces

Although problems connected with crawl spaces are dealt with in essentially the same manner as those associated with basements, dealing with the

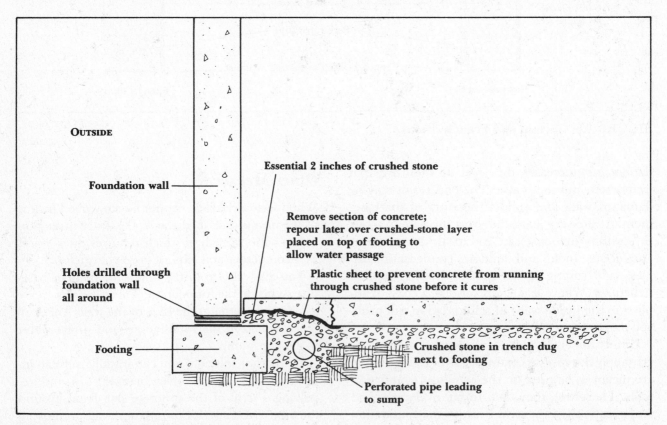

OUTSIDE

Foundation wall

Essential 2 inches of crushed stone

Remove section of concrete; repour later over crushed-stone layer placed on top of footing to allow water passage

Holes drilled through foundation wall all around

Plastic sheet to prevent concrete from running through crushed stone before it cures

Footing

Crushed stone in trench dug next to footing

Perforated pipe leading to sump

FIGURE 1.9 A subslab interior drain

former requires that you take one additional factor into consideration: bare soil.

Soil and other porous materials draw water up much like a blotter by a mechanism known as capillary attraction. This action can cause water to travel enormous distances. So even though the soil in your crawl space may appear to be dry, don't count on it. Crawl spaces contribute greatly to excessive moisture in many houses, and thus to the deterioration of floor joists, beams, subfloors, and roof sheathing.

All bare soil in the crawl space should be covered with 6-mil polyethylene plastic, tightly fitted against the foundation walls and weighed down with soil, bricks, stones, or any other nonorganic material. It is wise to carry the plastic up the walls to a point above the outside grade line, and to spot-tape it to the walls with duct tape. Use as wide a sheet of plastic as you can manage, and clean the dirt of sharp stones and other debris before laying it down, to avoid puncturing or tearing the plastic. Where seams are unavoidable, overlap the sheets by at least 1 foot, and spot-tape them with duct tape. Use care to seal as tightly as you can around piers.

If your crawl space has vents, as most do, you may want to close them and periodically give the crawl space the "nose test." If it smells good, keep the vents closed; this will make the crawl space warmer in winter, resulting in a more energy-efficient house, and prevent absorption of moisture by the wood in the warm and muggy weather of late spring and summer. However, if the crawl space smells musty, open the vents during cool, dry, and breezy weather. In warm climates where air conditioning is common, it is usually better to keep crawl spaces closed, but only if the bare dirt is thoroughly covered with plastic.

it is better to insulate the walls of a basement or crawl space than to place insulation between the first-floor joists. It is easier to insulate foundation walls than to work overhead with the floor joists. The former approach results in a warmer basement or crawl space, and it eliminates the need to insulate ducts and pipes. Moreover, it is cheaper to insulate the walls of a crawl space because there is much less area to cover. For walls up to approximately 8 feet high—the height of a full basement—less insulation is required than would be needed for the floor joists.

You must remember, however, that although insulating the walls of a foundation (or insulating between the joists of the first floor) reduces the amount of heat loss, it also allows deeper penetration by frost since there is less heat conducted through the foundation walls to the soil outside. This can be risky in locations where the soil around the foundation is expansive. The resulting expansion of freezing soil can exercise enough pressure on the walls to crack them and cause them to bow or shift. When in doubt, it is safest to insulate only the most vulnerable parts of the foundation, from the first-floor subfloor to 2 feet below the outside grade, leaving the bottom of the inside foundation wall exposed. This allows some heat loss to take place through the lower portion of the walls.

Continue your home inspection in the attic, with the assistance of the material presented in Chapter 2. Like the foundation, the attic is one of the first places problems make themselves known.

An Additional Consideration: Heat Loss

When you have solved all moisture problems and have achieved a dry basement or crawl space, you may want to consider insulating the walls, since foundations are responsible for a considerable amount of heat loss in a home. Generally speaking,

2

ATTIC

Out of sight, out of mind. That's the adage that generally applies to the attic, and as a result many homeowners never go into that area of their house. In truth, the attic is a very important part of a house and should be checked for potential problems.

Many problems in the attic can be corrected by a handy homeowner. The average do-it-yourselfer can easily handle jobs such as adding insulation, installing "fire-stopping" around a chimney, sealing open duct joints, and cleaning clogged insect screens on vents. But any project requiring modification of structural components, or modification of the existing electrical, plumbing, heating, air conditioning, flue, chimney, or fuel-gas piping systems, should not be attempted by anyone who does not have the necessary qualifications and, in some cases, licenses. All work should conform to the appropriate local codes, regulations, and standards. (If you intend to use a professional tradesperson, read chapter 11.)

Some of the problems found in attics require onetime correction; others require periodic checking and repair on an as-needed basis. Under normal circumstances, an annual inspection is recommended. If your home's attic does not have a provision for access, consider installing an access hatch.

When you check out your attic, you will need a flashlight, for obvious reasons. If your attic is the crawl type, with a very low ceiling, it's a good idea to wear workclothes, since clothing is likely to get soiled in the course of your inspection. It also makes sense to wear a dust mask over your nose and mouth to avoid breathing airborne particles of insulation or dust.

If the floor does not have a full covering—and floors in crawl attics typically do not—be very careful where you step. Walk only on the top of joists or on the catwalk, if there is one. Do *not* step between the joists; plaster or gypsum board usually will not support your weight, and your foot might poke through the ceiling of the room below. Be careful where you put your hands. There may be electrical hazards (such as open junction boxes), exposed nails, or a nest of bees or wasps.

This chapter gives you the information necessary to properly inspect your attic in order to identify (and solve) a variety of common and not-so-common problems associated with the area.

Roof Leaks

Even though your roof shingles may be in good condition, leaks can occur around the joints where a chimney, plumbing-vent stack, or attic ventilator projects through the roof. These joints, and those created where the surfaces of the roof meet at different angles or where the roof meets a wall, should have flashing. Flashing consists of thin strips (or a strip) of metal installed over the joint and under the roofing material so as to prevent leaks. Properly installed, flashing usually works well, but the joints of roof projections are still vulnerable to leaks and require occasional resealing. A roof is also vulnerable to leaks at points where accessories such as antennae or solar panels attach to it.

An ideal time to check the attic for signs of leakage is during a rain. Shine your flashlight at the underside of the roof and roof framing and look for a wet area, drip, or trickle of water. The sources for roof leaks are quite difficult to pinpoint because the water droplets can flow along the wood framing in the attic and drip a considerable distance away from their original point of entry. Nevertheless, if there is a leak, try to locate its origin by tracing water back to its source.

If you see evidence of an active leak around the joint of one of the roof projections, that joint will require resealing. *Note:* Any attempt to seal the joint from the attic area will be unsuccessful; repairs can be made effectively only from the roof. The best long-term solution is to flash or reflash the joint, but more often than not, the leak is sealed with asphalt cement. Sunlight tends to dry and crack asphalt cement over the years. Consequently, those joints should be periodically checked and resealed as necessary.

During an attic inspection, you can also look for leaks that originate at the top ledge of the chimney, an area that is often neglected. Most older chimney tops will have visible cracks, and rain will seep through the cracks and down the chimney into the attic. If this problem is occurring, the portion of the chimney passing through the attic will be wet or damp during a rainstorm. The solution involves getting to the very top of the chimney to install a new cement cap or at least applying roof cement to the cracked areas. These jobs should be done by a person who is used to heights and are not recommended for the average homeowner.

If leaks are found in areas other than around the joints of roof projections, they indicate the need for repair of roof shingles. (See chapter 3.)

By correcting a roof leak at this stage, you can prevent cosmetic damage to ceilings and walls that will occur when the leak reaches the habitable rooms below.

Ventilation

Moisture buildup, or condensation, in the winter and excessive heat buildup in the summer indicate the ventilation in your attic is inadequate.

Moisture buildup can cause plywood roof sheathing to delaminate. (Roof sheathing is nailed over the rafters and forms the deck for roofing paper, shingles, and other roofing material.) Wet insulation will not insulate. Moisture-laden wood framing—rafters, cross ties, and the like—will eventually rot, and water will stain and promote peeling of paint on walls and ceilings below. During your inspection, do not confuse wet insulation, wet wood framing, or even frost on the roof sheathing—all of which are generally caused by condensation of attic moisture—with a roof leak. If the condition is caused by a leak, you will find an active drip or wet spot during a rain, or an irregularly shaped stain caused by the drip on a dry day (in which case check the area again on a rainy day).

You can usually identify condensation problems. Moisture will tend to condense on the underside of the roof. This condition will be more prevalent on the slope facing north than on the southerly slope. If you are checking the attic on a cold winter day when the temperature is around 20 degrees F, you will find the area covered with frost. Eventually, the moisture causes a dark, mildew buildup on the underside of the roof. During the winter, moisture also freezes on the roofing nails, and during the heat of the day melts and drips onto the floor causing circular stains on the wood framing, insulation, and catwalks.

Even though many houses have a vapor barrier on the underside of the attic insulation, some moisture does tend to accumulate in the attic as a result of cooking, bathing, and using humidifiers. (Vapor barriers are discussed in detail later in this chapter.) Yet excessive moisture buildup has many causes. In houses with interior bathrooms, exhaust fans often vent the moisture-laden air directly into the attic rather than to the outside. As discussed in the preceding chapter, water seeping into basements and crawl spaces can create moisture problems in the attic.

Even when the attic is adequately ventilated, the air trapped in that area becomes very hot during the summer months. Its temperature can reach as high as 150 degrees F. Insulation between the attic "floor" joists does not prevent this high temperature from putting a considerable heat load on the rooms directly below and also on ducts and air-conditioning equipment that may be located in the attic.

Most attics have some means of ventilation, but quite often the effective ventilation opening is inadequately sized for the attic area. Attic vent openings are usually covered with louvers to deflect rain. Unfortunately, the louvers tend to obstruct the opening. With metal louvers, the free, unobstructed opening is reduced by about 40 percent; with wooden louvers, by about 75 percent. If insect screens are added, the unobstructed opening is further reduced.

When there is a vapor barrier beneath the insulation on the attic floor, there should be a free, unobstructed ventilation opening in the attic of not less than 1/300 of the square-foot area of the floor. And if there is no vapor barrier, it should be 1/150 of the floor area. Table 2.1 is a guide for determining the free ventilation area needed for an attic with a vapor barrier. If the attic doesn't have a vapor barrier, simply double the number.

If your attic is inadequately ventilated, you can correct the problem by either enlarging existing vents or installing additional vents such as a ridge, roof, turbine, gable, or soffit vent (see figure 2.1). A single vent opening in the attic, even when it satisfies the total area requirement, is not considered adequate. The best method for ventilating an attic is to use a combination of vents such as soffit *and* gable vents or soffit vents *and* a ridge vent (see figure 2.2). This induces a draft or convective air flow that exchanges attic air with outside air.

Whole-House and Attic Fans

Some houses have whole-house fans, mounted either in the attic floor or on the exterior side wall of the attic. In summer months, a whole-house fan can help cool a house at night by drawing hot air from the habitable rooms and expelling it through attic vents. With the downstairs windows open, a whole-house fan can replace indoor air with outdoor air every minute or two, assuming that the attic ventilation is adequate.

If there is a fan in your attic that is floor mounted, determine whether the vent openings from the attic to the exterior are adequately sized for effective operation. When the vent openings are too small, air pressure builds up in the attic, which means the system is not working effectively. Turn the fan on and, with plenty of windows and doors open, put the palm of your hand over a wall-mounted electrical switch plate in a room below the attic. If you feel air rushing onto your palm, the attic vent openings are too small and should be increased.

Whole-house fans generally have movable louvers in the exterior side wall, or gable end, of the attic and also in the ceiling below the attic. These open when the fan is activated and remain closed when the fan is off. When installing a whole-house fan, builders often remove the gable vents with fixed louvers and replace them with a larger-sized vent that has movable louvers. That practice creates a problem. During the winter months and during portions of the summer months when the fan is not operating, the louvers will be in a closed position and will thereby completely close off the vent opening, causing the attic to be inadequately ventilated. This problem can be avoided by adjusting the louvers so that even when the fan is not operating, they remain in a partly open position.

During the winter months, the louvers in the intake opening (the one to the attic in the ceiling) should be sealed shut to prevent humid air in the house from escaping into the attic and causing condensation problems. In addition, the intake opening should be insulated during the winter to minimize heat loss.

Finally, if there is no on-off switch for the fan in the attic within sight of the fan, one should be installed to prevent accidental operation when the fan is serviced. Check the fan belt to see if it is loose and should be tightened or if it is cracked or broken, in which case it should be replaced.

A fan that ventilates just the attic is called a power ventilator (figure 2.3). Although a power ventilator

TABLE 2.1 Free Area Ventilation Guide

SQUARE INCHES OF VENTILATION REQUIRED FOR ATTIC AREAS

Width (in feet)	20	22	24	26	28	30	32	34	36	38	40	42
20	192	211	230	250	269	288	307	326	346	365	384	403
22	211	232	253	275	296	317	338	359	380	401	422	444
24	230	253	276	300	323	346	369	392	415	438	461	484
26	250	275	300	324	349	374	399	424	449	474	499	524
28	269	296	323	349	376	403	430	457	484	511	538	564
30	288	317	346	374	403	432	461	490	518	547	576	605
32	307	338	369	399	430	461	492	522	553	584	614	645
34	326	359	392	424	457	490	522	555	588	620	653	685
36	346	380	415	449	484	518	553	588	622	657	691	726
38	365	401	438	474	511	547	584	620	657	693	730	766
40	384	422	461	499	538	576	614	653	691	730	768	806
42	403	444	484	524	564	605	645	685	726	766	806	847
44	422	465	507	549	591	634	676	718	760	803	845	887
46	442	486	530	574	618	662	707	751	795	839	883	927
48	461	507	553	599	645	691	737	783	829	876	922	968
50	480	528	576	624	672	720	768	816	864	912	960	1008

Length (in feet) is labeled on the vertical axis.

Using length and width dimensions of each rectangular or square attic space, find one dimension on vertical column, the other dimension on horizontal column. These will intersect at the number of square inches of ventilation required to provide 1/300.

is the least clear-cut approach to household cooling, one can be very effective in controlling heat and moisture buildup in the attic itself. If the attic floor is well insulated and has a vapor barrier, and if the attic is adequately vented, you'll gain little by installing and using a power ventilator.

A really overheated attic may harm roofing materials, shortening their useful life. Improving ventilation would help, and, in cooler climates, moisture ventilation is of concern during the heating season. If your attic has an inadequate vapor barrier, vents should help disperse moisture rising from the living area. But if attic layout makes it impractical to achieve adequate ventilation without a power ventilator, one may be worth considering.

For aesthetic reasons, the unit is usually mounted in the rear roof slope so that it is not visible from the front. In hot weather, it is normally activated at a temperature of 90 to 100 degrees F. In cold weather, the fan can be operated manually or controlled by a humidistat set to turn the fan on when attic moisture reaches a predetermined level. The fan in a power vent is sized just for ventilating the attic; it is not intended to ventilate the entire house.

The power vent should normally be operating during the warm days of summer. If it isn't, either the unit is malfunctioning or the thermostat is improperly set. On many units the thermostat is exposed and can be manually adjusted. But if the thermostat is factory set and not accessible, the unit

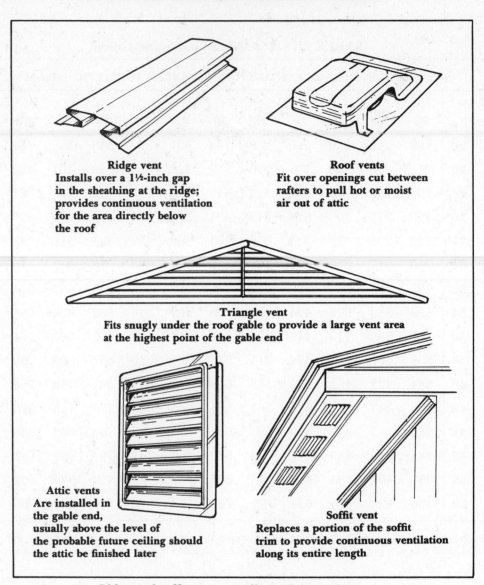

Ridge and soffit vents usually work in tandem.

FIGURE 2.1 Vents

will require professional maintenance. On cool but not cold days, you can usually check the power vent, assuming the thermostat is exposed, by lowering the temperature control setting until the fan is activated.

Insulation

All attics should be insulated to conserve energy. Adequate insulation reduces heat loss during the winter and heat gain during the summer. The amount of insulation needed for a particular house depends on its geographic location. You can find the recommended R-number (R = resistance to heat flow, or thermal resistance, of insulation) for the attic insulation in your area from the map in Figure 2.4. Bear in mind that although an unfinished attic is relatively easy to insulate, the first few inches of insulation yields the largest monetary saving; saving diminishes as insulation is added.

Measuring the thickness of the insulation will give you a rough idea whether you have enough. Add in the thermal resistance of the ceiling, R-2

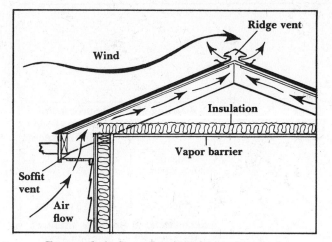

For good air flow, a combination of vents is recommended. A soffit and ridge-vent combination is shown; soffit and gable vents or gable and ridge vents can also be used.

FIGURE 2.2 Air flow using soffit and ridge vents

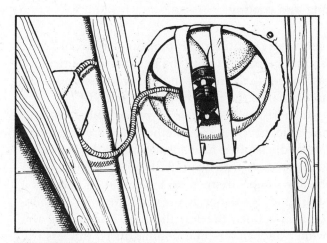

FIGURE 2.3 A power ventilator mounted between the roof rafters

for plaster and gypsum board and R-3 for acoustical tile. If insulation is inadequate, all you need to do is lay additional insulation over the existing batts to achieve the recommended R-number, since R-numbers are additive. Insulation comes in a variety of types and forms, so before purchasing additional insulation, check the label to determine its R-number. The label should clearly show the R-value and include a chart giving such information as length, width, and thickness of the insulation. If the label doesn't provide such information, don't

buy the product. The added insulation should be "unfaced," that is, it should *not* have a vapor barrier if the existing insulation already has a vapor barrier.

If you're handling the insulation yourself, wear protective clothing—gloves, a long-sleeved shirt, long trousers, dust mask, and safety goggles—to keep dust or stray mineral wool fibers away from your skin, lungs, and eyes.

In a crawl-type attic, the insulation should be installed between the floor joists, *not* between the overhead roof rafters. When the insulation is placed between the rafters and not between the floor joists, heat will escape from the finished rooms below into the uninhabited attic area—a clear waste of energy. But if the attic is large and high enough to contain one or more habitable rooms, and the ceilings of the rooms follow the roof pitch, the insulation should be placed between the roof rafters, and also on the unfinished side of the partition walls. To ensure proper ventilation and avoid condensation problems between the rafters, it is important to leave an air space between the top of the insulation and the underside of the roof deck.

If there is a furnace in the attic, the insulation should be located between the roof rafters. The insulation and the associated air space will help keep the roof deck cool. If the insulation is not between the rafters, heat from the furnace will warm the roof deck and melt the bottom layer of snow that has accumulated on the roof. This often results in an ice dam (see chapter 3).

If your house has soffit vents and the attic insulation is between the attic floor joists, check to see whether daylight is visible where the roof and floor meet. If daylight is not visible, the air passages for the soffit vents have been blocked by the insulation, making the vents ineffective. Reposition the insulation so that the air passages are clear. You can install prefabricated fiberglass or cardboard attic-ventilation baffles between the rafters in the attic eaves. These rigid baffles hold a space between the insulation and the roof deck to ensure good air flow.

The area over the hidden folding steps that provide access to some attics is often overlooked when insulating an attic. This area can be covered with a lightweight box constructed of rigid insulation. The box should be built so that it fits over the opening when the steps are in a closed position.

In general, insulation should not cover exposed

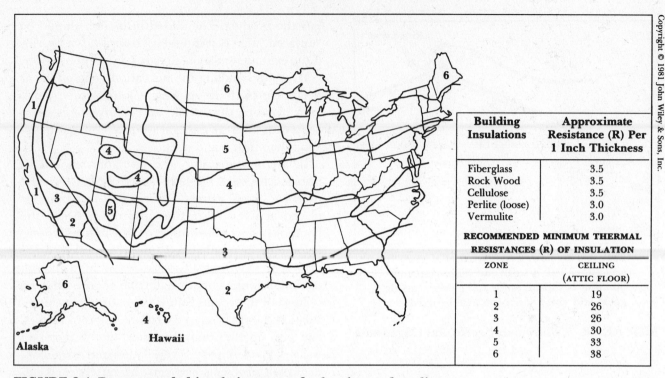

Building Insulations	Approximate Resistance (R) Per 1 Inch Thickness
Fiberglass	3.5
Rock Wood	3.5
Cellulose	3.5
Perlite (loose)	3.0
Vermulite	3.0

RECOMMENDED MINIMUM THERMAL RESISTANCES (R) OF INSULATION

ZONE	CEILING (ATTIC FLOOR)
1	19
2	26
3	26
4	30
5	33
6	38

FIGURE 2.4 Recommended insulation zones for heating and cooling

electrical components such as knob-and-tube wiring, transformers, and junction boxes (see chapter 7).

Some homes have "high-hat" light fixtures, the sides of which are recessed into the ceiling and exposed in the floor of the attic. When lit, the bulbs in the high hats generate considerable heat, which normally dissipates into the attic. But some contractors inadvertently cover the fixtures with insulation, thereby trapping the heat. This heat eventually causes the insulation on the electrical wires in the fixture to deteriorate, creating a fire hazard. If this condition exists in your attic, uncover the high hat and reposition the insulation around the fixture so that the heat can escape.

Improperly installed insulation creates another problem when it covers the vent outlet for a bathroom or powder-room exhaust fan. Many of these rooms have exhaust fans mounted in the ceiling venting into the attic. Quite often, insulation completely covers the units, which restricts the air flow and greatly reduces the effectiveness of the fan. When the exhaust fan services a powder room, which generates little moisture, all that's required is to move the insulation aside so that air can circulate freely. But when the exhaust fan is mounted in the ceiling of a bathroom, with a tub and shower

generating considerable moisture, a flexible duct should be connected to the exhaust fan outlet and extended up to and through the roof or a side wall to discharge the moisture to the outside.

If there are heating or air-conditioning ducts in the attic, check to see whether they are insulated. Metal ducts often have insulation on the inside, so tap the duct with your flashlight. If you hear a hollow sound, there is no insulation. If there is a dull thud, insulation is present. The more insulation on a duct, the less the heat loss during the winter and, in air-conditioning ducts, the less the heat gain during the summer. Generally, a minimum of 3 inches of insulation wrapped around the outside of the duct will substitute for missing internal insulation. When the duct is used for air conditioning, cover the insulation with a vapor barrier to prevent condensation from forming.

Vapor Barrier

There should normally be a vapor barrier between the floor joists of the attic to retard the movement of moisture from the heated rooms below to the unheated attic area. The vapor barrier should always be on the inside face of the insulation, between the insulation and the heated rooms of the building. When you are inspecting your attic, determine whether there is a vapor barrier. Lift up the insulation, and look on the underside. The vapor barrier either will be attached to the insulation or will be lying directly on the floor between the joists. Typical vapor barriers are 2- or 4-millimeter polyethylene sheets, asphalt-impregnated kraft paper, or aluminum foil.

If there is no vapor barrier, you have two choices. You can install a vapor barrier by removing the existing insulation, laying a vapor barrier down, and then replacing the same insulation. Or you can increase the unobstructed ventilation openings to 1/150 of the attic floor area (see figure 2.5).

On occasion, workers incorrectly install insulation with an attached vapor barrier facing the unheated, unfinished attic area rather than facing the heated rooms below. As a result, condensation can develop within the insulation. Correcting this problem is relatively easy. You can simply reverse the insulation so that the vapor barrier no longer faces the attic space.

When installing an additional layer of insulation, it is important to bear in mind that there should only be *one* vapor barrier. When you buy additional insulation, it should be unfaced—without an attached vapor barrier. If there is a second layer of insulation over the original insulation in your attic and it has an attached vapor barrier, you should either remove the vapor barrier or slit it with a knife or razor blade. Otherwise, the second vapor barrier can trap moisture and

cause condensation problems, such as decreased efficiency of the insulation or water stains on the ceiling below.

Fire Hazards with Chimneys

Most homes have a chimney that rises from the boiler or furnace room up to the attic and through the roof, where the exhaust gases from the boiler or furnace discharge harmlessly into the atmosphere. According to most building codes, as a fire-safety measure, there should be a minimum of a 2-inch clearance between the chimney and any wood framing. Wood normally begins to burn at temperatures of 400 to 600 degrees F. When it is subjected to high temperatures over a period of years, however, its ignition temperature can be reduced to about 200 degrees F. When wood framing is too close to the chimney, it may get as hot as its reduced ignition temperature. If this should happen, the wood will ignite and burn.

Although the clearance space around the chimney prevents a problem, it also creates one, because the open space around the chimney generally runs from the boiler or furnace room to the attic. In case of fire, that open space will draw the flames up to the attic and cause considerable danger and fire damage. Therefore, the open area between the chimney and the wood framing in the attic should be covered, or fire-stopped, with a noncombustible material such as sheet metal. This blocks the movement of air around the chimney and prevents that

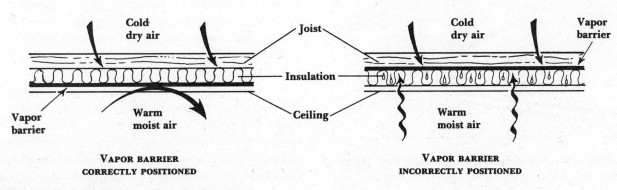

VAPOR BARRIER
CORRECTLY POSITIONED

VAPOR BARRIER
INCORRECTLY POSITIONED

FIGURE 2.5 Installation of vapor barrier

area from becoming a flue in the event of a fire in the boiler or furnace room.

If you have a fireplace or wood stove, annually check the section of the chimney that is exposed in the attic. After the fireplace or stove has been in use for several hours, go into the attic and feel around the chimney for hot spots and cracks. Look for leaking smoke. If you notice any of these problems, repairs should be made.

Air Conditioning

In many homes with central air conditioning, the blower coil (evaporator coil) is located in the attic. This is the unit through which the circulating air passes and becomes cool. In the process, the moisture in the air condenses and is channeled away from the unit through a drain line that often extends through the roof edge and terminates in a gutter. Sometimes, it runs down the side of the building where the water discharges onto the ground. Occasionally, however, an air-conditioning contractor terminates the drain line in a plumbing-vent stack (see figure 2.6). In most communities, this is an illegal connection. If this condition exists in your house, it should be corrected, either by the contractor who installed the system or by a plumber.

If the blower coil is located in the attic, there should also be an auxiliary drain pan underneath

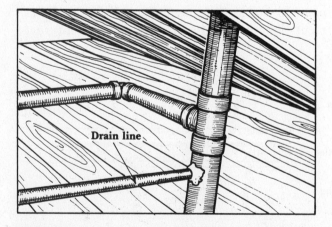

FIGURE 2.6 Air-conditioning drain line terminating improperly in plumbing-vent stack

the unit and the pan should have its own drain line. This back-up system prevents cosmetic damage to the ceiling below in the event that the main drain line becomes clogged. Unfortunately, many contractors leave the back-up system out or install it incorrectly. Check to make certain your unit has a pan and properly drained line. The auxiliary pan should have its own drain-line extension that discharges to the outside. It should not be connected to the main drain line, because if the main drain becomes clogged, the auxiliary drain will also malfunction.

If there are air-conditioning ducts in the attic, it's important that you occasionally check the joints for tightness of fit. Do this inspection when the air-conditioning system is operating, and feel around each joint. If any are loose or open, cold air will be discharging through them, and the condition will be very noticeable in the warm attic. You can correct the problem by resetting and resecuring those joints with duct tape.

Additional Checks

Sometimes kitchen exhaust fans have ducts that run up through the attic and vent to the outside. Sections of the exhaust duct are usually pressed into one another, and over the years a joint might open. Grease-laden kitchen air discharging from an open duct causes grease to accumulate on the wood framing and creates a fire hazard. Hence the exhaust duct should be inspected periodically. If a joint has opened, it should be resecured after resetting the duct sections.

Be sure to check the wood framing—rafters or trusses—for severely cracked sections, sagging sections, and a spreading of the rafters near the ridge. These problems, though uncommon, indicate a structural defect that should be evaluated by a professional.

Two attic-related problems can be detected from the habitable rooms just below the attic. If water stains are noted on the ceiling adjacent to one or more air-conditioning outlets, this generally indicates that the segment of the metal duct that runs from the main duct to the outlet grille is not insulated or is not insulated properly. The cool metal fitting causes moisture-laden summer air to condense and wet the ceiling in that area. In this case, cover the feeder section of duct with insulation that has a vapor barrier wrapped around the outside.

Where rooms directly below the attic have not been painted for many years, gray parallel lines spaced 16 or 24 inches apart may be noted on the ceiling. When there is insulation between the joists, during winter the temperature of the ceiling below the joists is cooler than the portion of the ceiling below the insulation—since wood is not as good an insulator. Depending on temperature and humidity conditions within the room, a slight condensation buildup can form on those strips of the ceiling below the joists. Over the years, that condensation holds dust, which builds up, causing the shadow lines. Painting the ceiling will correct the problem cosmetically, but after a number of years, the shadow lines will reappear.

A Timetable for Attic Inspection

As already stated, it is recommended that you inspect your attic annually. Most problems in an attic require only a onetime correction; other problems, such as open duct joints, roof leakage, a deteriorating fan belt, or clogged insect screens over the roof or gable vents, require correction on an as-needed basis.

If you have a whole-house fan or a boiler or fireplace where a portion of the chimney is exposed, you should inspect your attic more frequently—once each season. Insulation should be installed in the area around the attic fan's ceiling louvers before the winter, and removed in the spring. Fireplace chimney joints in the attic should be checked for signs of leakage when the fireplace is being used.

By following the recommended timetable for attic inspection, you'll be able to spot minor problems—and deal with them—before they develop into major ones.

3

ROOF AND GUTTERS

Roof materials and their associated parts, such as flashings, drains, gutters, downspouts, and skylights, cannot be ignored year after year and expected to be trouble-free. Proper maintenance can significantly extend the useful life of roofing materials and components, in particular the rain gutters and downspouts.

Many homeowners feel comfortable performing roof work and know how to safely use their own extension ladders. But if you don't like working from heights or handling an extension ladder, you should hire professional help.

You do not necessarily have to call a roofer for every job. Many roofing contractors are mainly interested in selling you a new roof and may charge you a sizable premium for small jobs. Use a reputable roofer when the problem involves hot tar coatings, broken roof shingles (especially slate shingles), worn-out roof flashings, and cement repairs to roof ridges, but other professionals may help with general roof maintenance. Local landscape contractors can be hired to trim tree branches off the roof, repair underground downspout drain systems, and restore grades after other repairs are made.

Roof Construction

The construction of your roof must conform to local building codes, in particular the standards for live-load capacity. Live load consists of any external force that might be applied to the roof, such as rain, snow, and wind. Sometimes codes mandate the types of material or minimum and maximum layers allowed, primarily to minimize fire hazards. Aside from aesthetics, roof design takes local codes and climate into consideration. Roofs with greater slopes, for example, accumulate less snow than low-sloped or flat roofs and therefore are the traditional choice in areas that receive a great deal of snow.

Various styles of sloped roofs include the gable, shed, mansard, hip, and gambrel (see figure 3.1).

Roof shingles, installed on sloped roofs, serve to drain off water. The most popular and most commonly used are asphalt-fiberglass shingles because of their reasonable cost, durability, and low maintenance. Other types of shingles used on sloped roofs include wood, slate, cement, and clay tiles, all of which are more expensive than the asphalt-fiberglass shingles. Metal roofing is another type of covering that is making a comeback on sloped roofs in many areas of the United States.

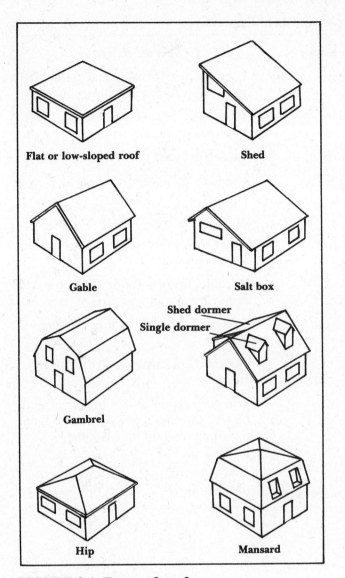

Flat or low-sloped roof

Shed

Gable

Salt box

Shed dormer

Single dormer

Gambrel

Hip

Mansard

FIGURE 3.1 Types of roofs

Low-sloped roofs and "flat" roofs require a different covering. They most often have alternating layers of roofing felts covered with roofing tars that together form a continuous sealed surface across the roof. Often the top layer of tar is imbedded with gravel to protect the tar from the ultraviolet rays of the sun and from erosion due to the weather. This covering is commonly called a tar-and-gravel roof, and all tar roofs of this type are known as "built-up" roofs, because the roof is built up into several layers.

Shingles should not be used on a low-sloped or flat roof because wind-driven rain, or even melting snow, can run under the shingle edges, or shingle tabs as roofers call them, and seep into the ceilings below. Homeowners often make the mistake of using shingles on the low-sloped roofs of storage sheds or additions built onto their houses. These roofs are prone to leakage.

Other types of materials used on low-sloped or flat roofs are mineral felt, or "roll," roofing, metal roofing, and newer single-ply membrane roofing. Roll roofing consists of one or two layers of roofing felt; tar is usually used to seal the joints. Membrane roofing consists of a single thin sheet of rubber or resilient plastic glued to the roof surface or mechanically fastened to the roof surface. A layer of smooth stones is often added for extra protection.

Table 3.1 lists various roof coverings and their average life expectancies. Asbestos cement shingles are not readily available anymore. Asbestos shingles can be identified by their brittle, grayish material and are normally rectangular. They are not known to present any hazard while undisturbed and in place on the roof, but if broken into pieces when replacing the roof, some asbestos fibers could become airborne. Since airborne asbestos particles can harm your health, do not sand and avoid breaking asbestos shingles. Replacing an asbestos shingle roof is a job for qualified and experienced professionals.

The other major parts of the roof system that you should inspect are the roof flashings, drains, gutters, downspouts, and skylights (see figure 3.2). Drains installed at the edges of flat roofs are called "scuppers" by roofers, and downspouts are often known as "leaders."

As mentioned in the preceding chapter, roof flashing is sheet metal or some other very durable material that is used to seal protrusions and joints in the roof where the shingles or the felts make a transition or change direction (see figure 3.3). Protrusions and joints that require sealing by flashing exist in areas such as the following: where the chimney comes up through the roof, where two different levels of the roof meet in what is called a "valley," where a roof surface butts up against a wall of the house or a dormer, or where a plumbing vent, fan vent, or skylight protrudes through the roof surface.

Flashed areas are a common source of roof leaks and therefore need periodic inspection and maintenance. Roof flashing is inexpensive to maintain

TABLE 3.1 Roof Types and Life Expectancy

Roof Type	Life Expectancy	Special Remarks
Asphalt shingles*	15–20 years	Used on nearly 80% of all residential roofs; requires little maintenance
Asphalt multi-thickness shingles*	20–30 years	Heavier and more durable than regular asphalt shingles
Asphalt interlocking shingles*	15–25 years	Especially good in high-wind areas
Asphalt rolls	10 years	Used on low-sloped roofs
Built-up roofing	10–20 years	Used on low-sloped roofs; 2 to 3 times as costly as asphalt shingles
Wood shingles*	10–40 years†	Treat with preservatives every 5 years to prevent decay
Clay tiles*	20+ years	Durable, fireproof, but not watertight, requiring a good subsurface base
Cement tiles*	20+ years	
Slate shingles*	30–100 years††	Extremely durable, but brittle and expensive
Asbestos cement shingles*	30–75 years	Durable, but brittle and difficult to repair
Metal roofing	15–40+ years	Comes in sheets and shingles; should be well grounded for protection from lightning; certain metals must be painted
Single ply membrane	15–25 years (manufacturers claim)	New material; has not yet passed the test of time

*Not recommended for use on low-sloped roofs
†Depending on local conditions and proper installation
††Depending on quality of slate
© ASHI

but may be very expensive to replace. Many homeowners mistakenly replace an entire roof to stop a leak when, in fact, merely recaulking a dried-out, cracked flashing seam would have solved the problem.

Inspection from the Ground

To provide the best preventive maintenance for your roof, you should inspect it twice a year, once at the end of autumn and once at the end of spring. But get into the habit of occasionally scanning your roof and the rain gutters and downspouts through-out the year, especially during and after big storms. Missing, cracked, or torn roof shingles can often be spotted from the ground, and should be replaced as soon as possible. By periodically scanning the roof you may spot minor defects—a disconnected downspout or a crack in flashing—before they lead to major damage. If possible, areas that have been inspected from the ground with the naked eye should also be gone over with a pair of binoculars. You will be able to make a better inspection of critical areas such as the chimney structure, the flashings at the chimney and valleys, and the small slots in between the roof shingles. You can even spot exposed nails used to secure the roof flashings.

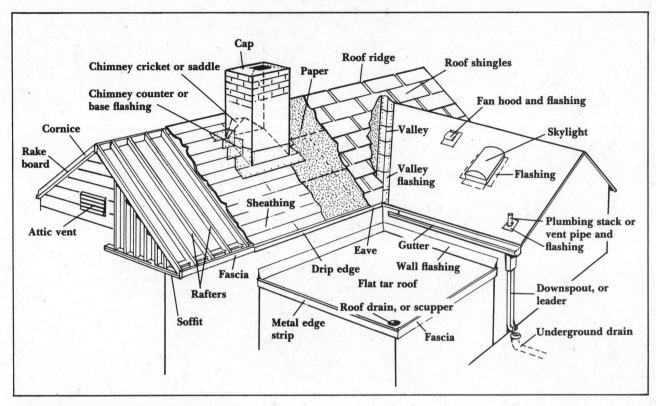

FIGURE 3.2 Major parts of the roof

There are several obvious potential trouble spots that you can see from the ground during your periodic inspections.

Trees

Tree branches that are scraping against or overhanging the roof should be trimmed, and that area of the roof checked for damage. Branches that overhang or have grown close to the chimney flues should be trimmed to avoid a fire hazard and to maintain proper drafting of the system.

Gutters and Downspouts

Regularly cleaning the debris out of the gutters will prevent water from spilling into the eaves, which can cause wood rot, paint failure, and wall damage. Water spilling over the gutters and collecting on the ground can cause damp or wet basement walls

(see chapter 1). Rain gutters that have leaves and twigs hanging out of them will need cleaning. Gutters and downspouts that have pulled loose or that have settled or sagged will need to be resecured and realigned. The correct slope for gutters is 1 inch down for every 10 feet of length to the downspout.

Lightweight plastic or metal screens can be installed over gutters to keep out leaves and twigs. They are designed to snap into the rims of the gutters. Many screening products perform with some degree of success, but you must continue to periodically inspect the gutters for clogging. This is especially true in colder climates where snow and ice can damage the gutter screens.

For flat-roof drains (scuppers) and for downspout connections at rain gutters, there are screen inserts that prevent leaves and twigs from dropping into the openings. These inexpensive devices are worthwhile products, but they themselves need frequent cleaning.

Splash blocks, which are troughlike cement or plastic trays about 2 feet long, should be set at

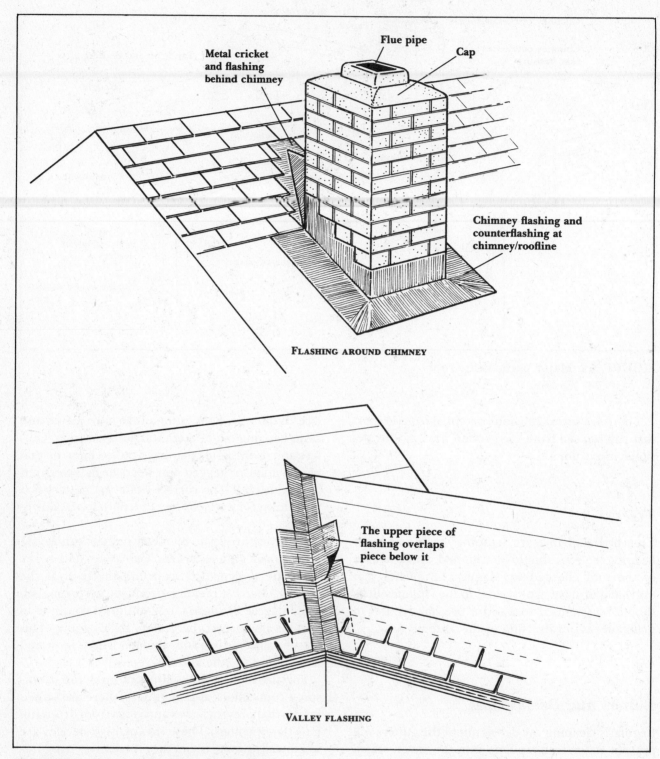

Flue pipe

Cap

Metal cricket
and flashing
behind chimney

Chimney flashing and
counterflashing at
chimney/roofline

FLASHING AROUND CHIMNEY

The upper piece of
flashing overlaps
piece below it

VALLEY FLASHING

FIGURE 3.3 Typical flashing installations

the bottom of downspouts to direct the water away from foundation walls (see figure 3.4). These inexpensive devices can be an important factor in maintaining dry basement walls (see chapter 1). Check splash blocks to ensure that their slope directs water away from the house. Angled downspout shoes should be made secure at the bottom of downspouts and pointed away from the house. Underground drains serving downspouts should be tested periodically for clogging by running water from a garden hose into them.

The Ridge

Roofs normally have a ridge cap installed along the ridges of the roof to seal the joint. From the ground, one can often spot areas along the ridge cap that are damaged or missing. Patching the ridges with roof cement is not an expensive job, but it is an important repair to make, and it does normally require a professional roofer to make the climb to the top of the roof. (Roof cement is a sticky, waterproofing compound.)

In the snowbelt, slate roofs often have copper ridge flashings which eliminate the need for periodic sealing. However, they can deteriorate, become loose, or fall off, and so their condition must be checked frequently.

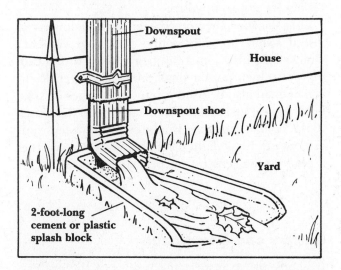

FIGURE 3.4 Typical splash block installation

Mildew and Moss

Moss and mildew may begin to grow on wood shingles or on flat tar roofs and should be treated to terminate their growth. Their tiny roots can penetrate roof materials and cause serious damage. To determine whether a discolored area is mildew, put a little laundry bleach on a cloth, take the cloth to the roof, and apply it to a spot. (Observe all the safety precautions given below for using a ladder.) If the spot lightens or disappears altogether, you are dealing with mildew and not just dirt. Don't simply attempt to scrub the spot off. You must apply or have someone apply a solution of one-part laundry bleach and three-parts water. Let the bleach solution dry completely, then scrub with some powdered detergent, and let the detergent solution dry on the wood.

Chimneys

The condition of the chimney structure, whether brick, stone, or metal, should be checked for such problems as eroding mortar, deteriorating chimney caps, and loose bricks on masonry chimneys or peeling paint or rust on metal chimneys. Loose or cracked chimney flashings are also a common problem. A small split in the flashing can create a leak that is difficult to trace if you are not aware of the cause. The flashing will have to be cleaned and resealed with asphalt roof cement or caulking sealant.

All these conditions can lead to water seepage through the chimney and into the roofing materials, causing roof decay and damage. Loose mortar and loose bricks should be repaired. A sound chimney cap of sand and portland cement will keep water from penetrating the bricks. A mason or chimney sweep should be called in to install new mortar in eroded mortar joints, seal (or "parge") top ledges with a coat of cement, and coat the structure with a silicone compound. Metal chimneys should be periodically painted with a rust-inhibiting paint to extend their useful life.

You may want to consider installing a spark arrestor screen or a weather cap, which will keep wildlife out of the chimney and enhance the draft. All metal chimneys must have a rain cap to prevent internal corrosion.

Antenna

From the ground, also periodically check the television or other antenna to make sure it is standing straight and that all its support cables are secure. If the antenna is leaning to one side, or is otherwise visibly shaky, it could mean that a support cable has pulled loose, leaving a hole in the roof.

Inspection Using a Ladder

If you are physically capable of using a ladder and feel comfortable with heights, observe the following safety precautions when inspecting a roof from a ladder.

Ladder Safety

Make sure your ladder is in good condition and that the rungs are solid and secure.

Always check for and keep the ladder away from any electrical wires when carrying it or placing it against the house. Do not wear leather-soled shoes; wear sneakers or other shoes with rubber soles to guard against sliding off the ladder or the roof.

Do not use a ladder or climb on a roof on a wet or windy day. Even flat roofs are slippery when damp or wet. Stay off slate, asbestos, wood, or metal roofs; roofs with ice, snow, frost, or fungus; and steeply sloped roofs. Even under the best conditions, be extremely careful at all times, especially near the edges of the roof.

Have a second person hold the bottom of the ladder whenever possible; make certain the ladder is secure and stable at the top and bottom. Keep children away from the area.

Flat Roofs

If you use a ladder, you can inspect the seams and surfaces of flat roofs for cracks, blisters, or bulges. Blisters and bulges on a flat roof may indicate that surface water has seeped into the inner layers of the roof through cracks or small holes. This condition may also be caused by excess humidity trapped under the roof or by improper adhesion of the roofing felts. To avoid damaging the roof, do not step on blisters and bulges.

The procedure for repairing a blister involves cutting through the middle of it, but not deep enough to damage the underlying felts (see figure 3.5). Roof cement is then forced into the cut, and the seams of the cut are closed against the roof with more cement, followed by a patch of metal flashing or roof felt. This patch is sealed down with roof cement around the seams.

If there is a gravel cover on your roof, check for bare spots and redistribute new gravel as needed. Flat roofs with built-up tar surfaces and no gravel should be recoated with hot tar every 3 to 4 years to extend the life of the roof. Some homeowners will recoat a flat roof themselves with a store-bought roof coating or sealer. These cold recoating compounds are better than no recoating at all, but they are not as effective as a recoating with hot tar. In addition, the do-it-yourself compound must be compatible with the tar already on the roof. The bitumen found in tar roofs and roof coatings is either coal-tar pitch or asphalt, and the two materials are not compatible.

On a flat roof, the homeowner can seal down any raised seams on roll roofing with roof cement. Cracked flashing joints can be repaired with a can of roof cement and a small, pointed trowel. Roof cement can also be used around the edges of skylights to seal up cracks in the seams, or in the joints of the skylight housing. But be careful to keep roof cement off the skylight plexiglass cover because the asphalt in the cement can permanently scar it.

Gutters and Downspouts

It is possible to inspect the insides of the gutters for any clogging or rusting by using a ladder.

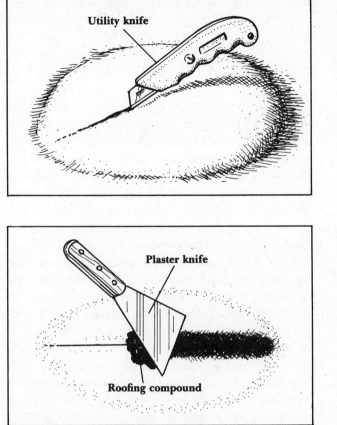

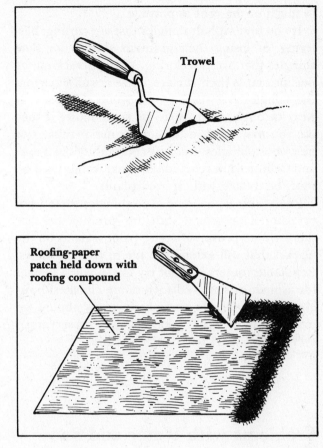

FIGURE 3.5 Repairing a blister on a flat roof

Leaves and foreign matter are the main causes of blockage. Inevitably, cleaning gutters is a messy business. Wear old clothes, and heavy, waterproof gloves to protect your hands.

Most rain gutters today are made of aluminum and do not rust, but on galvanized gutters rusting is quite common after about 10 years. The life of galvanized rain gutters can be significantly extended if the trough side is painted with a rust-inhibiting paint.

Flashing

With a close look at the roof flashing, you can determine whether the flashing joints are dried out or cracked. If so, they need sealing or caulking. Note, however, that properly installed flashing seldom needs caulk or sealant. These materials are normally used for repairing leaks and will fail in

time. The permanent, but expensive, solution is to install new flashing.

Flashing made of steel that is starting to rust should be painted with a rust-inhibiting paint to extend its life span. Any exposed nail heads should be covered with roof cement or caulk to prevent them from rusting. If you're not able to do this job, you might first try your painter. He or she will probably do a better painting and caulking job than the roofer, since roofers generally do not like to do such work.

Shingles

A ladder also makes it possible to closely inspect the roof shingles from the edge of sloped roofs. It is not a good idea to walk on the shingles. It can be unsafe for the inexperienced person, and it might damage the shingles. Use a ladder to view as much of the roof as possible.

If you find asphalt shingles that are curling, blistering, or losing their granular surface, or slate shingles that are discoloring, pitting, cracking, or peeling across their surface, these are all signs that the shingles are wearing out. Wood shingles may wear through, warp, split, or come loose; if they do, you may need to budget for major repairs or new wood shingles. In many communities in Texas and California, it is mandatory that woods used on roofs be treated with fire retardants.

Roofs with asphalt and slate shingles should not be painted or coated with any product because there are no proven effective paint sealants on the market that will extend the life of these shingles. Reputable roofers will not try to sell you a sealant for asphalt or slate roofs. In damp climates, however, wood shingle and shake roofs should be treated with special wood shingle preservatives every 5 to 7 years to extend their life.

Problems with Water and Snow

Many homeowners who suffer a roof leak believe it must be time to install a new roof and completely reshingle. More often than not, this is unnecessary. Even old, worn shingles seldom cause leaks unless they are actually torn or have holes through them. Most leaks come from cracks in the roof flashings, and these can be repaired with roof cement.

How can you best determine where the leak is coming from? If there is an attic space under the roof, this is the best place to start. As discussed in the preceding chapter, from the attic on a rainy day you should be able to see if water is leaking in from around the plumbing-vent pipes, the chimney structure, the underside of the roof valleys, the ridge vent, the roof-fan vent, or from the skylight housing. Leaks from any of these areas indicate problems with the flashing, not with the roof shingles. On the other hand, if you see water dripping off a nail shank through the underside of the roof sheathing, you probably have either a torn, cracked, or missing shingle, or a condensation

problem. Refer to Chapter 2 to learn more about attic inspections and water problems in that area.

Ice Dams

An attic inspection is also important when there is snow on the roof to determine whether an ice dam has formed along the eaves. Snow melting down the roof often refreezes and traps underneath it a pocket of water that is kept liquid by warmth from the attic (see figure 3.6). The trapped water backs up through the roof shingles and roof sheathing. Dripping water from ice dams can usually be spotted with a flashlight directed toward the eaves. This situation must be corrected, since extensive ice damming will cause damage at the ceiling line in the finished rooms below. Once a dam has formed, about all you can do until after the spring thaw is spread out plastic sheets in the attic eaves to catch the water and prevent it from damaging the ceilings below. From outside, get up on a ladder and carefully chip holes in the ice dam to let trapped water out, observing all safety precautions given earlier.

To reduce the risk of an ice dam forming in the first place, keep your attic floor well insulated to prevent household heat from escaping into the attic and melting the underside of the ice layer on your roof.

Ample soffit ventilation will also help prevent household heat buildup under the roof, and will keep the underside of the roof surface cold enough so that the ice will not easily melt. The sun should melt the snow and ice from the top down; you do not want the ice melted from the bottom up by household heat from the undersurface.

For hardy homeowners there is a relatively inexpensive tool called a snow rake that will remove snow from the eaves. It has a wide, lightweight blade and comes with long, extendable aluminum poles to allow you to reach the roof with the snow rake while standing on the ground. You can then pull or rake the snow off the eaves. The device does work, but you must be in excellent physical condition to handle the long poles attached to the

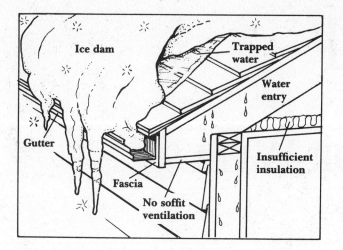

FIGURE 3.6 An ice dam

snow rake, and you must be very careful not to damage the roof surface.

When reroofing, you might want to consider installing a snow and ice shield on the lower 3 to 6 feet of the roof surface under the shingles.

Lessons for the Homeowner

By learning a basic lesson in roof structure, as well as acquiring an understanding of the common problems that may arise, you may be able to do minor repairs by yourself instead of hiring a professional. Even when you do decide to hire someone else to do the work, you won't be as likely to have a new roof installed just because a roofing contractor says you need one; you'll know enough to ask for a complete account of the whys and hows of the proposed repair before accepting that it is in fact necessary.

Another lesson has to do with safety. Roofs can be dangerous places to work; extension ladders can also present a hazard for the homeowner who uses them. By following the safety precautions provided in this chapter, you will minimize the risk of injury if you decide to do your own roof inspection and repair. But it bears repeating that if you have *any* doubts about your ability to work from a height, hire someone else to do the job.

4

EXTERIOR WALLS

The siding and trim of your home should be weathertight to prevent water damage and drafts. Peeling paint, damaged shingles, and open seams in siding and trim are not just unsightly; they invite serious problems. By providing early maintenance, you can avoid damage to the inner walls and, at the same time, give your home a well-kept appearance.

Exterior Wall Construction

The exterior walls of wood-frame houses consist of the following major components: framing, which includes both studs and wall sheathing; insulation; sheathing paper; and finally, the siding and trim (see figure 4.1). Proper upkeep of siding and trim ensures that the framing and insulation inside the wall will be protected from damage.

Walls are generally constructed with 2-by-4 wood studs placed 16 inches apart, measured from the center of one stud to the center of another. The studs are covered first with exterior-plywood or wood-board sheathing and then with felt building paper. Some localities allow 2-by-6 wood studs to be spaced 24 inches center to center, primarily to permit the use of thicker insulation. The newer the

home, the more likely that insulation of some kind was installed during construction.

Wall sheathing provides structural bracing for the wall frame, minimizes air infiltration, and usually provides a nailing surface for the siding and trim. In addition to plywood or wood boards, exterior fiber or gypsum board is also used as wall sheathing. In some homes, the siding—if made from plywood, for example—can provide both bracing and weather protection so that the sheathing and siding are one and the same.

Sheathing paper, which is asphalt-saturated felt paper or plastic impregnated paper, is used to prevent water from getting into the walls, particularly when it rains heavily or when rain is driven by strong winds. It is water- but not vapor-resistant, so that moisture can escape to the outside rather than remaining trapped in the inner walls. Sheathing paper also reduces drafts and cold air infiltrating the building.

Siding Materials

Many different sidings and trims are available; most of them have a life expectancy equal to that of the home itself. Nevertheless, sidings and trim

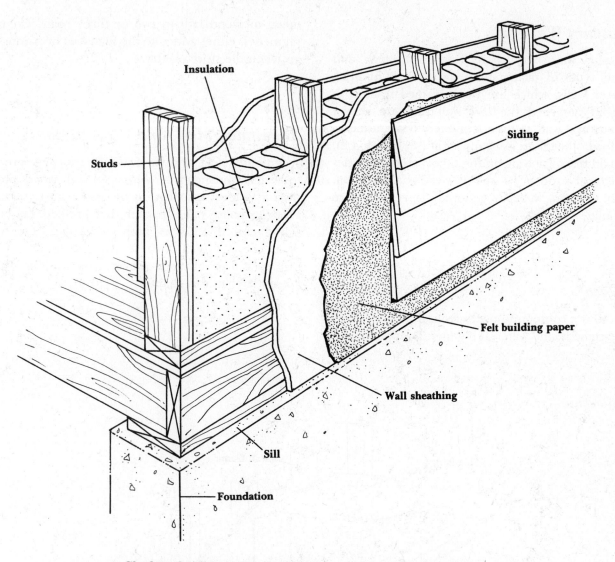

Clapboard siding is shown; shingles and other siding are nailed over the sheathing paper in a similar manner.

FIGURE 4.1 Typical wall construction

often fail much sooner because homeowners do not follow through with a regular maintenance program. No matter what the quality of the materials used, and regardless of what claims manufacturers make, the simple truth is that siding and trim do not last unless they are kept up well and on a regular basis.

Wood Siding

Wood siding comes as shingles, shakes, plywood panels, boards (applied horizontally or vertically), or hardboard. It is generally available in cedar, spruce, fir, redwood, and hemlock. Other kinds of wood may be used as thin veneers on exterior panels of plywood siding.

Masonry Walls

Masonry wall coverings include brick, block, and many types of facing stone. In the case of brick veneer walls, which are wood-framed walls with masonry attached, the brick wall is laid up against a structural wall, but is not bonded to it, and bears no load other than its own weight (see figure 4.2). A solid masonry wall, on the other hand, provides structural support as well as weather protection. Solid masonry walls are generally more expensive to build.

Stucco

Stucco is a compound made from fine sand, portland cement, and water. It is generally applied over metal or wood lath in two or three coats. Color pigment is either added to the final coat or painted on when the stucco is dry.

Aluminum, Steel, and Vinyl Sidings

Aluminum, steel, and vinyl sidings are considered to be maintenance-free compared with wood and masonry. Most installations include a fiber board or polystyrene panel backer that fits behind the siding and that serves both to insulate and to deaden noise. Each of these sidings does have its own special problems, however, which will be discussed later in this chapter.

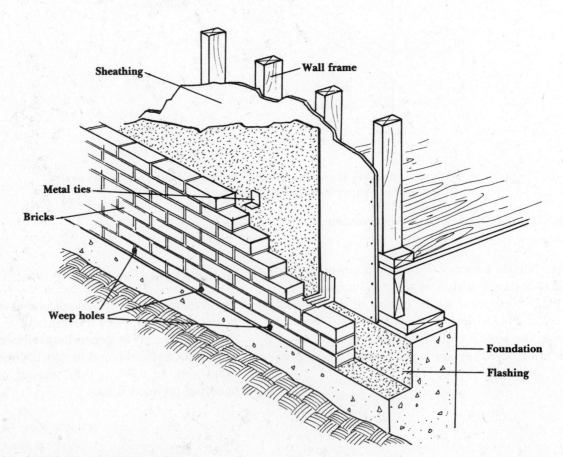

FIGURE 4.2 Brick veneer construction

Miscellaneous Materials

Other siding materials include asphalt siding and asbestos cement shingles, often referred to as composition shingles. Generally, asbestos shingles are no longer in use for siding on homes, and asphalt shingles, although still in use, are not much in demand. Because the airborne fibers associated with asbestos constitute a health hazard, removal of asbestos shingles is a job for qualified and experienced professionals. Do not sand and avoid breaking such shingles.

Exterior Trim

Exterior trim includes the various moldings and finishing materials used around the windows and doors; protective covers for edges, joints, and corners; and the materials used to cover soffits and fascias. Like siding, exterior trim functions primarily to shield the building from weather intrusions, thereby preventing decay of and damage to framing, insulation, and interior walls and floors.

Trim also comes in a variety of materials, but is usually chosen to match the material of the siding, wood, metal, and vinyl being the most common.

Looking for Trouble

No matter what type of siding and trim is on your exterior walls, you can follow the same inspection procedures. Keep in mind, though, that damage and deterioration show up somewhat differently on wood than on brick, block, or stone. You are mainly interested in detecting areas where water may have penetrated the lines of defense. Consider water in any shape or form—rain, melting snow, or ice—to be your chief adversary.

During your inspection, try to be systematic in your approach in order to avoid duplicating your efforts. Work your way around the house, making notes of any damage and deterioration that you can observe; later, you'll want to make an in-depth evaluation. Start from the top and work your way down each wall to cover the entire surface area of

the exterior systematically. Give yourself plenty of time for this task. Look carefully for defects, and if necessary probe the wood with a blunt tool—an old screwdriver will suffice—to determine whether there has been damage. Pay particular attention to walls facing south and southwest because they are the ones that are much more exposed to sun and to variations in temperature, and thus are apt to deteriorate more quickly.

As you visually inspect the upper areas of the wall, be sure to scrutinize the siding and trim near the roof drainage system—valleys, gutters, and downspouts—since a great deal of damage and decay is related to poor drainage. Adjacent trim, like fascia and soffits, is greatly affected by the elements of nature, particularly at joints and seams (see figure 4.3). Be certain to closely examine joints and seams for vulnerability to water penetration.

To make the inspection process of the upper portions of the exterior walls a little easier, use binoculars or a ladder. As is true with any work on a ladder, always use extreme caution and follow the safety procedures given on page 36. Another way to get a closer look at your upper walls might be by looking out of your upper-floor windows. (You may want to combine a close look at the upper walls with the inspection of windows and doors, the subject of the next chapter.) Again, use caution and common sense. As you check for defects, look around for potential causes as well. Sometimes, overgrown vegetation is the culprit. Make a written note of any pruning that has to be done.

Portions of the exterior walls that are shaded and receive little or no sunlight are often prone to fungus and mildew growth. You can usually identify growths by the dark and blotchy patches that they leave on wood. Refer to the maintenance section of this chapter for ways of controlling and eliminating fungus and mildew.

As you work your way down the walls, examine window and door trim for open seams and joints (see chapter 5). Check the drip caps and flashing over each window and door. If your windows have shutters, be sure to look them over thoroughly for decaying wood or damaged vinyl. Wood shutters often start to sag; eventually their slats will loosen and drop out. If you see signs of sagging, you can correct it early on with metal corner braces.

At the sides and corners of the house, very care-

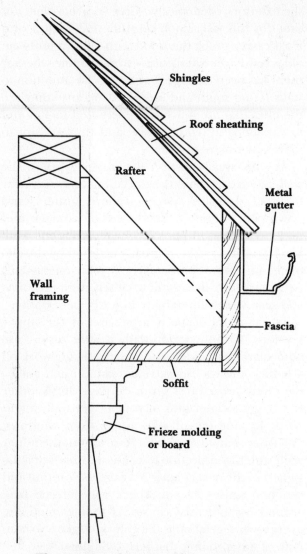

Shingles

Roof sheathing

Rafter

Metal gutter

Wall framing

Fascia

Soffit

Frieze molding or board

The gutter can be secured by a strap hanger that is fastened to the roof sheathing, a bracket hanger fastened to the fascia, or a spike-and-ferrule driven into a rafter.

FIGURE 4.3 Trim at the edge of the roof

fully inspect for open seams and missing trim. Note any damaged areas that could allow water to penetrate. Pay attention to areas where different materials meet, wood siding and brick veneer, for example, since joints, gaps, and damaged flashing are an open invitation for moisture to get in. Make a written notation of all areas that need to be caulked (see page 46).

Sight along the length of each exterior wall during your inspection tour. If you notice sags or

bulges and you cannot determine the cause, call in a professional for help. The cause could be something as typical as stucco pulling away from walls, for example, or it might be a more serious structural defect that needs repair.

Wood Siding

Wood siding of any kind is prone to insect attack as well as to water damage, so look closely at areas where the wood is close to or in direct contact with the soil. These areas may also be overgrown with vegetation, and shaded areas are especially susceptible to rot. Use an awl or old screwdriver to probe for areas of decay or infestation. Record the locations of any soft and rotted wood and plan for immediate remedial maintenance work. Regrade the soil away from wood. As mentioned, it is very good maintenance practice to keep low wood siding and trim at least 6 to 8 inches away from the ground.

In general, inspect wood for peeling or blistered paint; warped, split, or cracked shingles; delaminating plywood; the dark stains of mildew; or buckled boards—all of which indicate water damage. The sources of such damage may be indicated by open seams in siding and trim, open gaps at outside corners, missing or damaged caulking, loose, missing, or rusty nails, or holes needing to be reputtied.

Make a note as well of areas needing a general cleaning and those stained by rusty nails or chalking paint.

Brick, Block, and Stone

With masonry materials, you'll be inspecting principally for open cracks in the materials themselves or at their joints, and for weakening mortar. Using an old screwdriver, scratch along joints where mortar appears to be loose to test for sandy, crumbly mortar—the signs of weakening. These joints will need repair (see page 48). Make a note of efflorescence stains for later cleaning (see page 45–46). Look for missing or badly damaged bricks, blocks, or stones. Here too, a bulging wall could indicate a serious structural problem.

Stucco

If your home has a stucco exterior, inspect it for cracks, holes, or crumbling sections. If the stucco is painted, look for areas that are peeling; carefully inspect the adjacent trim for open gaps and seams. If you find significant damage, try and find the source of the water penetration, and suspect damage to the underlying wall.

Aluminum, Steel, or Vinyl

Inspect aluminum and steel siding for dents and scratches, and steel siding for corrosion. Metal siding should have a ground connection at each corner of the house. If the siding is painted, is the paint peeling or stained at areas that should be caulked? Vinyl siding is subject to cracking. Inspect all siding for open seams and joints.

Asphalt or Asbestos Shingles

Asphalt or asbestos shingles can tear, chip, or crack. Look for peeling paint or damaged coatings and finishes, missing or damaged caulking at joints, loose seams, and missing and loose nails. Everything should be well sealed and weathertight.

Although it is safe to carefully replace a few asbestos shingles yourself, never sand and avoid breaking them, as mentioned, since this can create airborne asbestos particles that can harm your health.

The Trim

Inspect all trim carefully since this area is likely to develop serious problems with water penetration. The trim should have no open gaps or joints. Probe suspect wood with a blunt screwdriver to check for soft or decayed spots. With vinyl trim, determine whether the cracks go all the way through the material. Corrosion on metal trim may also indicate water damage. Look for peeling paint; missing, loose, or rusty nails; and sections of trim that may be completely missing.

Maintenance Routines

Your routine maintenance should comprise periodic cleaning, caulking, painting or staining, and simple preventive repair jobs on an as-needed basis. Since this is not a book about repairs so much as maintenance, you may need to turn to other sources for more complicated repair tasks. You should have no difficulty finding do-it-yourself information in bookstores or libraries.

Cleaning

One of the simplest maintenance chores for your walls is to clean them periodically. A simple hosing down of your siding and trim to remove accumulated grime and dirt will help keep these surfaces in good shape. For very dirty surfaces, you can use a carwash brush that attaches to a hose, or wash with a solution of water and trisodium phosphate (TSP), which can be purchased in hardware and paint stores. TSP is caustic and can irritate your skin and eyes. Always follow the instructions on the label carefully and wear a long-sleeved shirt, rubber gloves, face mask, and safety goggles when using it. Cover any plantings beneath where you're working.

Mildew and efflorescence are two substances that should also be cleaned off your exterior walls. Mildew is a fungus that thrives in moisture and loves to grow on shaded walls. To remove it, mix one-part household liquid bleach with three-parts warm water. Scrub the affected areas with this solution and a stiff brush. For best results, let the solution soak in for 15 minutes or so and then rinse the wall thoroughly with a garden hose and let dry. Scrub again with water and powdered detergent, if necessary, and rinse thoroughly. When using house-hold chemicals, wear protective clothing and safety goggles and cover nearby plantings, as stated above.

Efflorescence is the powdery residue of mineral salts left on masonry walls after water has evaporated from them. The first step in removing it is simply to brush it off with a stiff fiber or wire brush. If this doesn't work, try vigorous scrubbing with a regular household cleanser. You may have to try a commercial wash, but use one only as a last resort and follow all precautions on the label. Avoid using muriatic acid. It is a very hazardous substance. Its vapors are harmful, and it can burn your skin and cause serious, permanent damage to your eyes.

Caulking Openings

Make caulking and sealing open joints, gaps, and seams in the exterior wall coverings a priority in your maintenance program. Openings will allow moisture to creep into your building; drafts, water, and perhaps even insects can easily penetrate them. Since even the best-quality caulking compounds dry out eventually, you should look for areas that need to be resealed.

Figure 4.4 shows the most common exterior areas that need periodic caulking. Caulking open seams is a simple maintenance chore. Applying caulk so that it fills the joint smoothly and evenly is an acquired knack, but anyone can learn it. The only tools that you need are a caulking gun and a putty knife. Be sure to caulk around wall vents, electric meters, and pipe and hose bibbs, in addition to caulking around trim.

The following tips can help you do a neat and effective caulking job:

- A clean surface is essential. Remove old caulk and be sure joints are dry. (Only latex caulk can be used in damp joints.)
- Cut the cartridge nozzle on an angle, so you can slant the cartridge for better visibility and control. The nozzle cut should just span the average width of the joint you're trying to fill (⅛- to ¼-inch in diameter should be sufficient).
- Poke the nozzle into sections of the joint wider

than the nozzle so that the caulking fills the gap from the deepest part of the joint up to the surface. Rough-fill really wide, deep gaps with inert filler such as oakum or wood strips and the caulk.
- Press the nozzle firmly over joints and *push* the caulk ahead of the tip to force caulk deep into the crevice.
- Remove excess caulk and smooth with a moistened stick, putty knife, or rubber-gloved finger. After you develop some expertise in using a caulking gun, you may be able to eliminate this final step.

Maintaining Paint and Stain

Exterior paint or stain is the first line of defense against decay and deterioration. If you keep the paint on your house in good condition, and joints and seams well caulked and wall surfaces clean, you will greatly reduce the odds of wood decay and moisture penetration. Although both paint and stain are important for the upkeep of your home, they are not without problems. Paint will blister, peel, flake, and check, among other things; stain, with the passing of time, will fade and erode. What follows, then, is a closer look at why exterior paints and stains fail and how to remedy some of these shortcomings.

Paint blisters and peels because the temperature was too high at the time the paint was applied, because some moisture was trapped under the paint or because moisture is trying to work its way out from the inside. Temperature-related blisters are not very common; to prevent them, never paint in direct sunlight or when it is very hot outdoors. Moisture-related blisters, on the other hand, develop much more readily, and the only way to avoid them is to locate and eradicate the source of moisture itself before painting.

Blistering and peeling paint is usually the result of improper bonding to the underlying surface. Most likely, the surface areas were dirty, wet, glossy, or not appropriately primed when paint was applied. Paint will blister and peel when indoor moisture pushes outward through the walls. Such vapor movement, if excessive, can even peel paint

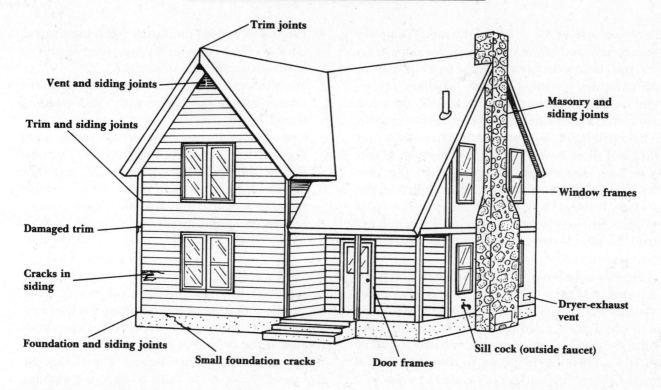

Trim joints

Vent and siding joints

Trim and siding joints

Masonry and siding joints

Damaged trim

Window frames

Cracks in siding

Dryer-exhaust vent

Foundation and siding joints

Small foundation cracks

Door frames

Sill cock (outside faucet)

FIGURE 4.4 Areas that need caulking

right down to the bare wood. To avoid such unsightly surfaces, clean, sand, and prime all areas before painting them. At the same time, check your home's requirements for ventilation, and, if necessary, provide additional roof ventilation or a whole-house fan to control the indoor moisture (see chapter 2).

Paint will most likely come off in flakes once the surface is heavily cracked. Flaking can also occur if a thin coat of paint was applied on top of a thick coat or vice versa. Large sections of paint often will flake off and leave bare, exposed siding and trim behind. Proper surface preparation and paint selection will help prevent such problems in the future.

In some white paints, chalking is a built-in, self-cleaning property designed to keep siding looking fresh. Such paints tend to develop chalky, white powder on the surface. This powder washes away, taking dirt and mildew with it. If the chalking process is excessive, however, the pigment in the paint washes away so fast that the siding is exposed rather than covered with a protective coat.

Chalking paint above brick siding is undesirable because the paint might wash down and stain the

brickwork. To avoid that, use a non-chalking white paint over brick work.

Other things that can go wrong with paint include alligatoring, wrinkling, and crawling. These usually occur because the paint was applied incorrectly, the surfaces were not properly prepared, or too many coats of paint were applied. If the paint on exterior walls shows such shortcomings throughout, you should remove the paint all the way down to the bare wood. However, this is a job that goes far beyond general maintenance, for it involves heavy scraping, sanding, priming, and then repainting, all of which are very time consuming and strenuous and best left to a professional.

Some stains do not develop the defects characteristic of paints. The major upkeep chore is to restain every 5 to 7 years—as required—to liven up the fading color and restore the stain's weather-protection properties.

The tools needed for maintenance painting jobs are a simple assortment of brushes, scrapers, sandpaper, and ladders. With larger jobs, it may be necessary to rent scaffolding and power sanders at a local rent-a-tool company or hardware store. Be sure to follow both the manufacturer's recommendations as well as the advice of the rental company for the safe and efficient use of such equipment.

Good surface preparation is the best way to stave off paint deterioration. On wood surfaces, scrape and sand the damaged sections. Make certain you remove all loose paint. Wash the affected areas with a mild detergent, hose off residual loose paint and dirt, and allow the surface to dry completely. Then reset any loose or popped nails, putty over the holes, allow the putty to dry, and sand flush to the surface. Prime all bare areas. Last, apply two coats of paint. By preparing a surface well, you will extend the time between full-scale paint jobs, which are costly and time consuming.

Steel or aluminum sidings first have to be wire-brushed or sanded to remove rust and other types of corrosion. Then the bare areas should be primed with metal primer and repainted with a matching color. To avoid future corrosion, you may also want to add a chemical retardant to the paint, if the manufacturer has not already added it, when you touch up metal siding or trim.

Simple Repairs

Maintenance also includes simple repairs that will help you avoid costly replacements in the future. You can fill small holes in wood siding or trim, for example, with wood putty, available at paint and hardware stores. Allow the putty to dry thoroughly, sand the surface until it is smooth, and then stain or paint to match the siding or trim. (The touch-up probably will not match the rest of the trim.) For larger holes, you will need several layers of putty before you finish off with paint or stain.

The most common maintenance repair job for masonry walls such as brick, block, and stone is to repoint them. Pointing up brick is a process of re-placing damaged and weak mortar joints with fresh mortar. Follow these steps for weathertight mortar joints:

- Clean out loose or deteriorated mortar with a chisel or tuck-pointing tool. Remove the smaller particles by flushing with a hose or by using a wire bristle brush and water.

- Prepare premixed mortar by following instructions on the label (you can purchase mortar at hardware stores or lumberyards).
- Wet the areas to be filled in and then press the mortar into the open joints with a tuck-pointing trowel.
- Use a jointer tool to finish off the joints. After about 10 minutes, clean excess mortar from the face of the brickwork with a brush, and then give the joint a final pass with your jointer tool to make sure that you smooth both horizontal and vertical joints evenly.

The following are two important points to remember when pointing up brickwork. First, match the new mortar mix with the original mortar. If in doubt about this, check with a mason or a masonry-supply store. Second, do not seal up the weep holes located at the bottom of brick walls because these openings allow moisture to escape. The average do-it-yourselfer can easily learn to do small pointing jobs. If extensive areas need work, it's best to leave the job to a mason.

Hairline cracks in stucco can easily be concealed by painting over them with a coat of latex paint. Larger stucco cracks, however, should first be filled with latex caulking and then painted over. Small holes in stucco can also easily be repaired. First, remove all debris from the hole and make sure that the bonding underlayment is intact. If the wall lath or wire mesh is damaged, replace it with the same material, if possible, or with an appropriate sub-stitute. Next, thoroughly wet the area of the hole to be patched so that the new patch will adhere to the older and dryer portions. Finally, mix up a batch of stucco patch compound (available at most building-supply stores) and use it to fill the hole. Be sure to follow the manufacturer's directions for mixing and use. Holes larger than 6 inches wide should be left to a professional mason.

Dents in metal siding can be repaired by pulling them out, using a self-tapping sheet metal screw to pull on. Start by drilling a small hole into the center of the dented area. Drive in the screw, but in order not to split the metal, attach a rubber ferrule (cap) or two washers to the screw's head as a spacer. After you have driven in the screw, grasp the end of it with a pair of pliers and *gently* pull until the dent has flattened out (see figure 4.5). When the dent is gone or nearly gone, remove the screw and apply aluminum or steel filler to the hole you just made with the screw. Once the filler has hardened, sand it until the surface feels smooth and then touch it up with paint.

Persistent Problems

Sometimes, even after the best of cleaning, caulking, and overall maintenance, you will find that paint persists in peeling or that masonry walls go on cracking and crumbling. In cases such as these, before you consult a professional, you may want to

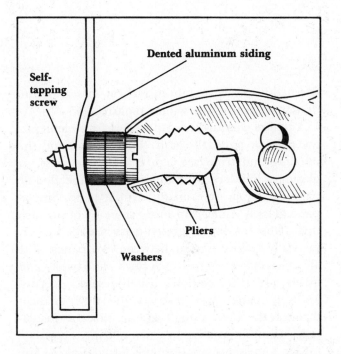

FIGURE 4.5 Removing a dent from metal siding

investigate on your own to determine the exact cause of the problems. They may be the result of outside conditions. In particular, faulty roof drainage can cause backups that affect both the interior and exterior walls and cause deterioration of siding and trim. Be sure to reread Chapter 3 for an explanation of roof and roof drainage systems. But remember that not all damage and deterioration of exterior walls and trim is caused by water from the outside. Sometimes, visible defects on the outside can be traced directly to inadequate moisture ventilation or vapor barriers indoors.

Stucco or brick walls that persist in cracking may do so because there are structural problems in the foundation or frame of the building. Review Chapter 1 for maintenance recommendations on foundations and advice on what to look for when inspecting for cracks. Bulges and sags in masonry walls usually indicate deteriorated mortar in solid masonry or damaged ties between brick veneer and the house framing. More often than not, these bulges affect only the areas involved, so that the rest of the house is sound. Keep in mind, though, that these visible signs of damage may indicate the need for major repairs.

Visible exterior rot may be the symptom of much more serious conditions that are hidden. Be sure to further probe with your screwdriver any suspicious-looking areas to determine whether the problem is more than superficial. If your screwdriver goes through the siding or trim into the sheathing and interior framing, you have a serious problem on your hands, and an impartial inspector, engineer, or reputable contractor should be called in to determine the full extent of the damage.

In fact, whenever your detective work does not uncover the source of problems that are persistent, consult with a professional for advice and perhaps repair service as well.

5

WINDOWS AND DOORS

Windows provide natural light and ventilation, and doors, of course, give access to and from the home. If properly designed and maintained, windows and doors can fulfill their function yet provide protection from the elements and security against intrusion. From an aesthetic point of view, they often add beauty, symmetry, and character to a building, and thereby increase its value.

Windows

Windows are usually classified by the materials from which they are made and by the method by which they open. For example, if you have a window that is made of wood, has two sections that move up and down, and has a single pane of glass in each section, it would be called a wood, double-hung, single-pane window—a design familiar to everyone. Windows are made of wood, steel, aluminum, vinyl, vinyl-clad wood, aluminum-clad wood, or vinyl-clad aluminum. Some windows are made with a thermal-break, which is a strip of insulating material that separates the interior part of the window from the exterior. The function of the

thermal-break is to minimize heat loss and condensation during the winter months.

A typical window is composed of four elements: the glass or pane, the sash, the framing, and the molding and trim (see figure 5.1). The glass, or glazing as builders call it, can be single pane, double pane, or triple or even quadruple pane. Single-pane glass is usually no more than $\frac{3}{16}$ of an inch thick, whereas double-glazed glass is made by hermetically sealing dry air between two panes. The air space may be $\frac{3}{8}$ to 1 inch thick. The triple- and quadruple-pane windows use the same process. Multiple pane glass restricts the flow of heat through the glass, using dead air space as insulation. As an alternative to extra glazing, manufacturers sometimes apply a special coating to the inside pane of double-glazed windows. Glass treated with the coating is called low-emissivity or "low-E" glass. Low-E glass reflects radiant heat and helps keep the house warm in winter and cool in summer. Low-E glass is almost as effective as glass with a third or fourth pane.

The sash is the unit that slides or pivots when you open or close the window. The sash includes the glass and its supporting framework, which consists of horizontal pieces called rails, vertical pieces called stiles, and bars that separate the glass panes

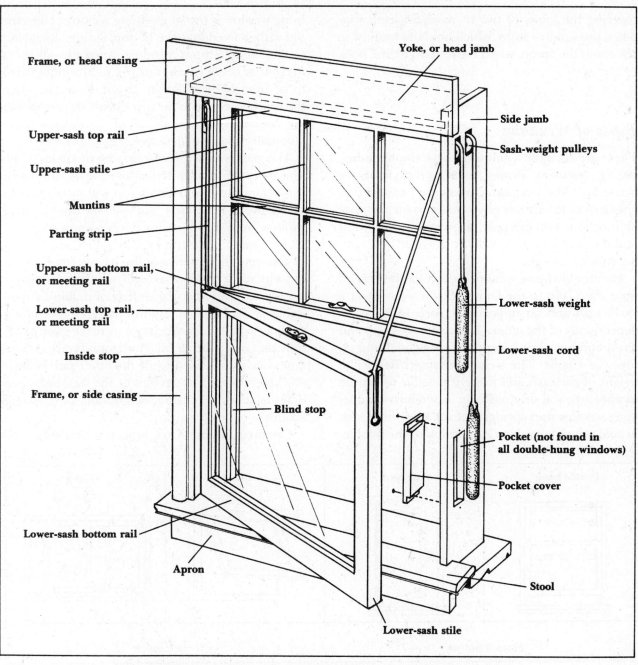

Frame, or head casing

Yoke, or head jamb

Upper-sash top rail

Side jamb

Upper-sash stile

Sash-weight pulleys

Muntins

Parting strip

Upper-sash bottom rail, or meeting rail

Lower-sash weight

Lower-sash top rail, or meeting rail

Lower-sash cord

Inside stop

Frame, or side casing

Blind stop

Pocket (not found in all double-hung windows)

Lower-sash bottom rail

Pocket cover

Apron

Stool

Lower-sash stile

An older window with sash weights is shown. Most modern windows have tubular-spring or spring-tape balances.

FIGURE 5.1 Parts of a typical double-hung window

called muntins. Locks and lifts, weather stripping, and in some cases sash cords, chains, springs or hinges are also considered part of the sash.

The exterior window frame consists of a sill, a side jamb, a head jamb, strips called stops that hold the sash in place, and the exterior casing or framework.

The interior window moldings include the stool, which rests on top of the sill; the right, left, and top casing, or trim; the mullion casing, which is the trim covering the joints of two or more adjacent windows; the window stops, which hold the window in place, and the apron, which is nailed under the stool.

Types of Windows

There are six basic window designs: double hung, sliding, casement, awning, fixed, and skylight (see figure 5.2). Many manufacturers use various combinations of the six designs to suit a particular style or function. For example, a greenhouse window found in many kitchens will use the fixed and awning window design.

The double-hung window, which has been used since the 1700s in the United States, consists of a lower sash and an upper sash, each working independently of the other. The sashes move up and down and are often balanced by weights hung on ropes or chains. The weights counterbalance the weight of the sash and make it possible to set the window open at any position. A modern double-hung window uses springs on each side of the sash to hold the sash in place. A variation of the double-

hung window is the single-hung window. Here the top sash is fixed and the bottom sash is movable.

The double-hung window generally allows a maximum of 50 percent of the total window area to be used for ventilation. In other words, when the window is open as far as it will go, the two sashes are doubled up and only half of the window space is actually allowing air to pass through.

The glass within the sash may be subdivided into a number of smaller individual panes supported by the muntins. Sometimes you will hear builders or architects refer to a "six-over-six double-hung window" or a "six-over-one double-hung window." If, for example, the upper sash has six small panes of glass and the lower sash also has six small panes, the window is called a six over six. Some windows use clip-on grids to give the effect of multiple panes.

The second type of window design is the sliding or slider window, in which two or more glass panes slide past one another on a horizontal track. Sometimes one sash is fixed while the other sash is movable. Here again, 50 percent of the total sash area is available for ventilation in a double-sash, sliding window.

Casement windows are hinged at the sides and

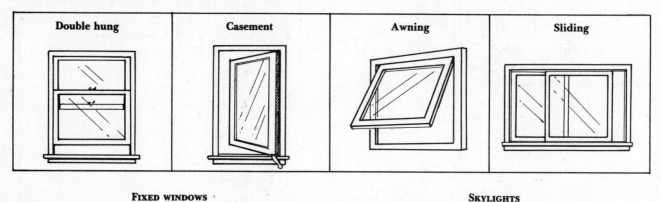

FIGURE 5.2 Types of windows

swing outward or inward. The sashes are opened and closed either by a crank or push bar mounted on the frame or by a handle fastened to the sash. Fully 100 percent of the total window area is available for ventilation.

The awning window contains one or more top-hinged, outward-swinging sashes. When open, the sashes extend out at an angle and resemble an awning. There are four variations of the awning design: the top-hinged window, similar to the awning window except that it opens inward instead of outward; the utility window, sometimes called the hopper window, hinged at the bottom and usually found in basement windows; the jalousie window, which contains a series of horizontal glass panes that open outward in unison; and the transom window, which is sometimes found above interior doors. All types of awning windows provide 100 percent of their total sash area for ventilation.

The fifth window design, the fixed window, consists of a frame and an immovable sash. Examples of fixed windows are the picture window, the decorative bay window, and the quarter-round window often found in the gable end of an old house on either side of the chimney. Fixed windows, as the name implies, provide no ventilation.

The last type of window is the roof window, or skylight. The skylight itself can be fixed, with a flat, pitched, vaulted-ridge, pyramid, or domed design; or a vented window equipped with a manual or power-operated sash. To keep rain out of the building, the vented skylight does not open as widely as the awning window. Therefore, the effective ventilation area for the vented skylight is considered to be no more than 50 percent of the total skylight area.

Doors

Exterior doors must be designed to protect the homeowner from the elements and intruders, reduce heat loss, and provide privacy for the homeowner. Interior doors must provide privacy and cut down sound transmission within the home. Exterior front doors are commonly 36 inches wide and 1¾ inches thick, whereas secondary exterior doors—side or rear door or the door from the house to the garage—and interior doors are commonly 27 to 32 inches wide and 1⅜ inches thick, although many other sizes exist. Most doors measure 6 feet 8 inches to 7 feet high.

A door is held at the frame by metal hinges or tracks. The frame consists of a head jamb, two side jambs, and stops against which the door closes. Exterior doors also have a sill or threshold made of wood or aluminum that slopes down to shed water away from the entry.

Doors are made from a variety of materials and come in several basic types: flush, panel, batten, patio, and garage (see figure 5.3).

The flush door is flat on both sides and can be either a solid-core door or a hollow-core door. The solid-core flush door is made of wood blocks or composition material formed into a solid piece. It provides greater security, better insulation of heat and sound, and more fire resistance and rigidity than the hollow-core flush door, which is veneered plywood with a core of wood cross braces or cardboard strips.

Another variation of the flush door is the metal-clad exterior door, consisting of steel-faced panels with an insulating core, and sometimes a thermal-break, a strip of insulation that prevents any part of the outside steel panel from touching the inside steel frame. This keeps the outside cold from being transmitted directly to the inside frame, eliminating condensation.

Panel doors consist of frames enclosing flat or raised plywood or solid wood panels, and may be used as either exterior or interior doors. Exterior panel doors may substitute glass for wood panels.

Batten doors are made of boards secured by diagonal or cross bracing and nailed with screws or clinched (bent-over) nails. They are usually found in cellars, sheds, and other places where appearance does not count. It is difficult to make them water- and weather-tight.

The sliding patio door has a main frame, usually two glass panels, single pane or double pane, and one screen panel. The door slides on tracks. Security bar locks overhead and/or foot bolt locks at the base of sliding doors are desirable.

Garage doors are usually made of metal, wood, or fiberglass. They can be hinged, sliding, or overhead doors. The overhead type can be a roll-up

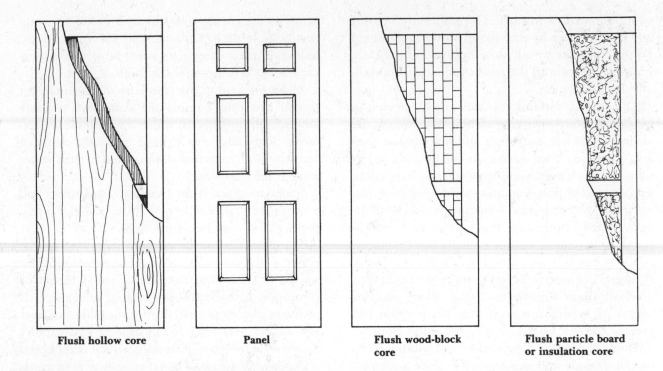

Flush hollow core   Panel   Flush wood-block core   Flush particle board or insulation core

FIGURE 5.3 Typical types and styles of doors

door with sectional panels or a swing-up door that moves up in one piece. Garage doors should have a gasket—a type of weather stripping—along the bottom edge to keep water out.

Storm Windows and Doors and Screens

Single-pane windows are a major source of heat loss in a house. Since glass is not a good insulator, heat travels through a pane of glass very easily. Storm windows, however, can reduce heat loss through windows significantly. The three basic types of storm windows are storm sashes, storm panels, and combination storm and screen windows.

The storm sash, often called the seasonal storm window, fits over the entire window and is attached to the frame of the window by means of hooks or clamps. Seasonal storm windows are common in older houses.

The storm panel is a single pane of glass edged with wood, metal, or plastic. It is placed over the sash of the window and is held in place by clips or screws. The storm panel can be attached on either the inside or the outside of the window. Whereas the storm sash is attached to the outside window frame and effectively shuts the window for the season, a window with storm panels can still be opened.

The combination storm and screen window has storm and screen sashes installed in a single frame, which can be aluminum, steel, or solid vinyl. The frame is permanently attached to the exterior frame of the primary window by means of screws and should be caulked along the top and sides between the storm frame and the window frame to reduce air infiltration. Never caulk along the bottom of the storm-window frame. This blocks the weep holes put there to allow water to escape. Double-track and triple-track combination storm and screen windows are the most typical, with the storm sashes and screens arranged on the tracks in various ways.

Storm doors are a must for all entrances in cold climates. But a storm door may not be appropriate where a metal-clad entrance door is used, since the heat buildup between the storm door and the metal-clad door may be so great that any plastic decorative panels on the metal-clad door will actually melt.

Caulking and Weather Stripping

As discussed in the preceding chapter, caulking seals cracks and gaps around windows where frames meet exterior siding material and around doors where the trim meets the exterior siding. Sealing cracks and gaps reduces the rate of heat loss by air infiltration and prevents penetration by rain and subsequent condensation. Caulking cracks and gaps around windows and doors will also lengthen the life span of the latter as well as produce more comfortable living conditions. All caulked joints need periodic inspection and repair because of the constant expansion and contraction of materials caused by seasonal changes in the weather.

Weather-stripping materials are available in a variety of forms. Weather stripping is usually installed on windows where the sash and frame meet and on doors where the door and jamb meet along the sides and top. Weather stripping is made of bronze, aluminum, steel, and rubber or plastic strips. Less durable weather-stripping materials include adhesive-backed foams, felt strips, and foam rubber with wood backing. Weather stripping needs to be periodically inspected and repaired, particularly the less durable forms, which have a tendency to deteriorate quickly when a window or door is used often.

Making an Inventory of Problems

The following inspection plan should be carried out about once a year. But you may discover that you can find the time to inspect all windows and doors thoroughly just once. If so, you should still check caulking and weather stripping each year without fail, and repair cracked panes, broken hardware, stuck windows and doors, and other problems as needed. You can combine your inspection of the doors and windows, but they are discussed separately. As mentioned earlier, during your interior walk-through to inspect windows and doors, you may want to look out upper-story windows and check the upper portions of exterior walls.

Windows

Assemble a pad of paper, a pencil, an old screwdriver, a tape measure, and a flashlight. Begin by inspecting the windows from the inside of the house. Try to be systematic: Draw a rough floor plan as you go from floor to floor and room to room. Work from the top down, moving around each room in a consistent direction. Number the windows sequentially and write down each window type, the dimensions of both the panes and the frames, and any problems encountered.

Open and close windows to check for ease of operation. Sticking windows may be caused by the presence of moisture, in which case you must reseal the window or open weep holes to allow moisture to escape. Or the cause may be excessive layers of paint between sash and frame, which can be cut through with a stiff putty knife or window zipper. (A window zipper is a special tool with serrated edges.) With storm windows the problem may be dirt or corrosion in the tracks. Clean the tracks thoroughly, and apply graphite or silicone lubricant. Look for cracked or broken panes that need replacing, and make note of chipped, cracked, or missing putty where the glass pane meets the sash. (Note that a cracked pane of glass sometimes indicates a problem with the settling of the house structure.) Check the sash, frame, and molding for peeling paint, which might only be a sign of age, but which could be caused by an intrusion of moist air or rain from poorly caulked windows or from a lack of weather stripping.

On wood frames look for cracks and rotting sections by carefully probing suspicious areas with a screwdriver, noting the depth of the damage. Rotting sashes, frames, or moldings—or mildewed, insect-infested wood—are also signs of the intrusion of moist air or rainwater through the window. The cause of the problem must be corrected, and the rotted elements may have to be replaced.

On double-hung windows, repairs would have to be made on broken or missing sash cords or sash springs, loose or binding sashes, and loose, broken, or missing hardware such as locks and lift handles. On steel casement windows look for cracked panes, rusting or bent frames, stuck sashes, and broken hardware.

Whenever you are dealing with insulating-glass

windows with hermetically sealed double panes, be alert for various signs that the seals are faulty (see figure 5.4). Moist air entering the space between the panes will produce water droplets or cloudy films in between the panes. This indicates that the pane's seal has broken. The solution is to replace the entire pane of glass, which is an expense that may not be justified. The problem is cosmetic; the broken seal does not affect the pane's insulating properties. Check storm and screen windows for condensation, cracked panes, torn screens, and blocked weep holes. And to mention the obvious, if you feel a draft through a closed window, you have a problem that needs correction.

Unless you examined each window when you checked the siding and trim, repeat your window inspection from the exterior of the house. Using your screwdriver, probe the sash, frame, and trim, where you can reach it. Note any peeling paint, rotted wood, or insect infestation. Termite-damaged wood will have a dirty honeycombed look to it. Damage from carpenter ants will show up as smooth, bored holes in the wood. Recheck windows for cracked, loose, broken, or missing panes and for cracked, chipped, or missing putty.

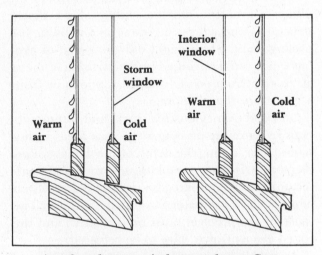

A sash and storm window are shown. Condensation in double-glazed windows occurs under similar circumstances. If the interior sweats, cold air is entering around a poorly sealed storm sash. If the exterior sweats, warm air is escaping around an interior window that is not sealing properly.

FIGURE 5.4 Condensation on windows

Most of the problems you are likely to encounter will be related to deterioration of seals, caulking, or weather stripping, and the solutions will be to reglaze windows and to recaulk or weather-strip panes and sashes. This will improve insulation and control moisture and is a job you can usually do yourself.

Doors

Combine your inspection of all doors with your tour of the interior and exterior windows. Make a note of the type and the dimensions of each door. Check exterior doors for ease of operation, and inspect all jambs, thresholds, and molding for peeling paint, cracks, and rotted wood, all of which indicate a moisture problem. Examine locks, handles, and hinges for loose, broken, or missing hardware. If the door has a window, look for cracked or broken panes and chipped, cracked, or missing putty. If the door features a double-glazed window, water droplets or cloudy areas between the glass panes indicate a faulty seal. Cracked or missing caulking between the doorjamb and threshold and the exterior siding can be found by probing with your screwdriver. Constant opening and closing of an exterior door will eventually wear down or loosen plastic and foam weather stripping, so watch for deterioration of weather stripping around the doorjamb and at the bottom of the door and top of the threshold.

For garage doors, check for ease of operation by lifting the door a few times. Listen for squeaks and rattles; feel for dragging or binding. Look for broken, cracked, or missing windowpanes, or chipped, cracked, or missing putty or wood strips. Probe with your screwdriver for wood rot or insect damage. Has the gasket at the bottom of the door deteriorated? Wood rot and insect damage, again, indicate moisture is getting to the wood. For electrically operated garage doors, check the safety reversing mechanism by holding the door handle as the door closes to verify that the mechanism works.

And finally, for interior doors, check for ease of operation; look for dragging or binding caused by carpeting, loose hinges, or misaligned components.

Screen and Storm Doors

Keep a record of the type and size of your storm doors. Check them for ease of operation. Make certain the spring or hydraulic device closes the door fully. Look for loose hinges, misaligned parts, a loose bottom-adjustment piece, or faulty weather stripping. Replace cracked, broken, or missing panes. Slide the glass up and down or in and out. Make sure all panes are made of safety plate or plexiglass to protect against injury from shattered glass. For wood storm doors, probe for cracked, broken, or rotted sections. For combination screen and storm doors, look for loose, broken, or corroded sections. Screens should be checked for torn sections and holes.

Your "Punch" List

After you complete the inspection, use your notes to create a "punch" list, which is a list of things to do:

• Repair cracked, loose, or broken panes as needed, and repair any chipped, cracked, or missing putty.
• Scrape and paint peeling window sashes, frames, and molding, as well as door frames.
• For double-hung windows, repair or replace broken sash cords or sash springs, loose or binding sashes, and loose, broken, or missing hardware.
• For steel casement windows, seal or replace rusted or bent frames and repair inoperative hardware.
• For double-glazed windows and doors, identify faulty seals and replace entire pane units as needed.
• Repair or replace any storm windows that have missing glass, cracked, broken, or corroded sections.
• Patch screens or replace the screening.
• Recaulk cracked or loose caulking.
• Repair damaged weather stripping.

In summary, your principal maintenance task for windows will be to maintain their integrity. Glazing and caulking are jobs that many homeowners can do by themselves without difficulty. (If you must use a ladder, observe all safety precautions given on page 36.) Malfunctioning doors can be more difficult to fix. A few repair suggestions follow; a good home-repair book can provide you with detailed repair procedures.

Before removing and planing a hinged door that won't close, try tightening the hinges. If you must remove the door, try resetting the hinges before you plane the edges. Concentrating repairs on the hinges usually solves the problem.

Another common problem with doors is a poor fit within the door frame. A door that is too small will show daylight around its edges when closed, or you will feel drafts. If weather stripping won't solve the problem, you may have to replace the door. Swollen or warped wood will have to be planed and refinished. Metal doors and their frames can bend, making repair difficult. Replacement may be called for. Door locks and associated hardware can be tricky to fix; it's usually a good bet to hire a licensed locksmith to install and repair them.

If a hinged garage door sags, tighten all the hinges. The door may not be square, requiring the installation of wood or metal braces. If an overhead garage door won't open smoothly don't attempt to fix it yourself—powerful springs may be involved. Make certain the door's safety-reverse mechanism works well. Have a professional check it.

Most door and window problems are caused by water and moisture. Read the chapters on foundations, attics, and roofs to learn more about the possible effects of too much moisture and about how to control moisture in your home. You may also want to check with your local utility company to find out whether it provides free or inexpensive energy audits. Not only will the inspector recommend procedures for door and window improvements, but he or she will often supply caulking, samples of weather stripping, draft stoppers for electrical outlets, and other energy-saving materials.

6

INTERIOR WALLS, CEILINGS, AND FLOORS

The finished interior walls, ceilings, and floors of your home form a cosmetic shell concealing from your view the structural frame, the plumbing, the electrical circuitry, heating and cooling ducts, and other building components that would be unsightly or hazardous if exposed. For this reason, a careful examination of the interior surfaces of your home can sometimes uncover symptoms of more serious problems in one of its basic systems or components. For example, water damage to a wall might be traced to a plumbing leak or a loose rain gutter; cracks might indicate a problem with the framing or the foundation. You'll be looking for such clues as you inspect interior surfaces; refer to other chapters of this book as you try to trace problems to their origins.

Interior Walls

There are two kinds of interior wall: load bearing and nonload bearing. A load-bearing wall is part of the structural frame of the house and supports a ceiling, roof, or floor above itself. A nonload-bearing wall is often referred to as a parting wall or curtain wall, since it is not designed to support such loads (see figure 6.1). Nonload-bearing walls can sometimes be removed during remodeling without affecting the structural integrity of the

house, but such walls usually contain wiring, plumbing, or heating ducts, a circumstance which complicates such work. Distinguishing a load-bearing wall from a parting wall can be done only from the attic, crawl space, or basement, and is best left to an inspector, engineer, or builder.

Wallboard, which is also called gypsum board or drywall, is the most common wall covering now in use because of its ease of installation and low cost (see figure 6.2). In homes constructed before the 1950s, smooth plaster over lath was the standard for interior walls and ceilings. Lath is the backing to which plaster is attached. Lath may be composed of narrow wood strips or wire lattice attached to the studs, or it may be similar to gypsum board. Gypsum board lath has holes so that the plaster coating will penetrate and lock into the lath when dry. Plaster walls are still built today, but they are very expensive.

Drywall and plaster provide a smooth surface for paint or a solid surface for other materials such as ceramic tile or wallpaper.

Ceilings

Ceilings may be flat and level, or they may be pitched to follow the roof line. Pitched ceilings

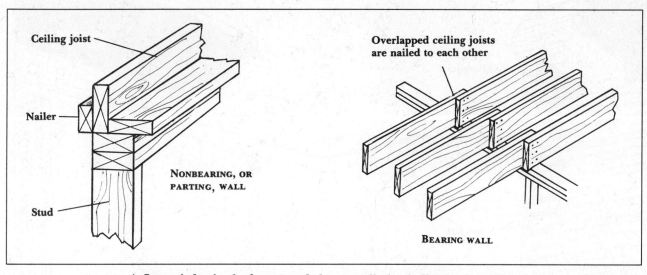

A floor girder in the basement below a wall also indicates the wall is load bearing.

FIGURE 6.1 Typical attic framing for bearing and nonbearing walls

are called vaulted or cathedral ceilings. Ceilings may have gypsum board, plaster, or wood as a covering over the ceiling joists. Older ceilings are sometimes covered with various types of acoustical tile.

Suspended ceilings are exactly that—lightweight panels suspended on a metal grid of interlocking tracks. The panels, as well as the drop-in lighting fixtures, are easily removed for repair or remodeling, which makes this type of ceiling very popular in commercial buildings.

Another common ceiling is made of interlocking tiles installed on wood furring strips or glued directly to the old ceiling. These tiles are often used to cover a previously damaged ceiling and can be an effective remodeling choice.

Wood ceilings and exposed beams are often found in ranch and contemporary style homes. (Some old houses and many adobe homes also have exposed beams.) These materials need little maintenance other than occasional vacuuming of cobwebs and removal of hardened sap. If your home has a room with exposed wood ceilings or beams, pay close attention to roof maintenance (see chapter 3). Even the slightest leak will cause damage that may cause permanent discoloration or require expensive bleaching or even replacement of the damaged wood.

Floors

Traditional floor coverings include hardwood, wall-to-wall carpeting, ceramic tile, and resilient sheet or tile flooring. Examples of more unusual and expensive floor coverings are polished marble, granite, and terrazzo. Defects in floor coverings can indicate movement—settling, heaving, and shifting—of the building's structure, as well as moisture problems.

Under the finished floor, there are three common types of subfloor construction: wood, concrete, and mortar beds. (See figure 6.3.) Wood subfloors are strong and flexible. They are easily prepared for carpeting and resilient flooring, but they must be adequately strengthened against movement before installing nonflexible tiles.

It's easier to install tile and stone coverings over a concrete slab than over wood. Unfortunately, the rigidity of concrete may be a drawback because after putting down an inflexible floor covering, even minor movement causes cracking. Concrete floors in basements and garages should not have any floor covering that could absorb gasoline and oil, which increases the risk of fire.

Some floor coverings serve a particular need. Resilient sheet flooring has become popular in kitchens and bathrooms where wetness prevails and frequent cleaning is necessary.

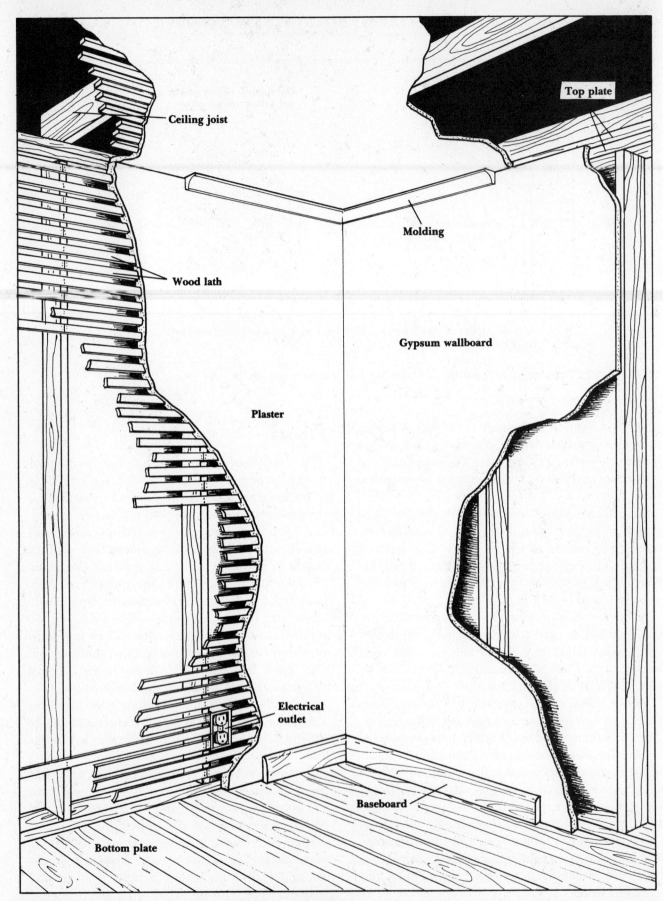

FIGURE 6.2 Plaster and wallboard wall construction

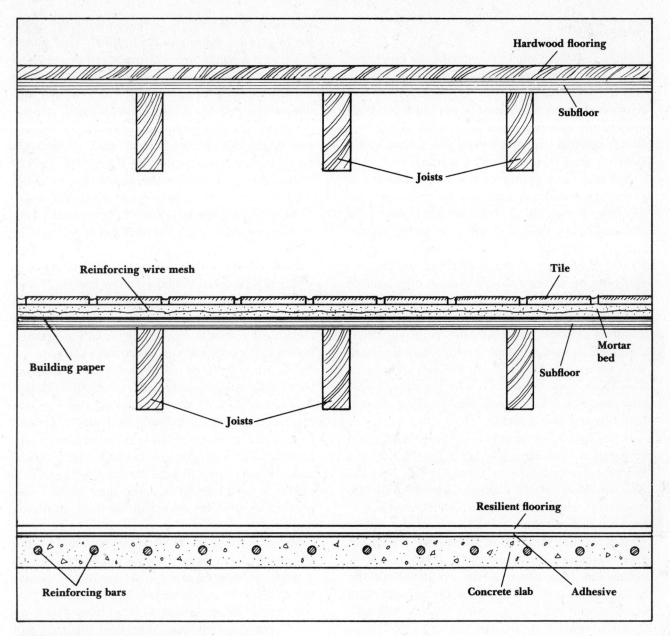

FIGURE 6.3 Typical floor construction

Taking a Fresh Look

To inspect walls, ceilings, and floors properly, you'll have to pay careful attention to what your senses of sight, touch, and smell tell you. You'll also have to train yourself to spot small changes over time, and to act promptly when you discover a problem.

Inspection of the interior surfaces of your home, as implied above, should be a continuous, year-round process, with a really thorough going-over

about once a year. It's recommended that you read chapters 1, 2, and 3 before inspecting interior surfaces. Have handy a flashlight, a scratch awl, a stepladder, a tape measure, a 4-foot level, pliers, a magnifying glass, and a notepad and pencil. You may wish to combine your inspection of the floors, walls, and ceilings with your inspection of the interior windows and doors (see chapter 5).

Sagging

As you go from room to room, look for bowing or sagging ceilings, walls, or floors. Sight along walls and use your hands as well. In good light, a bow in the ceiling will be obvious from floor level. Walk around the room, and use your sense of touch to find problems. Use your level if you suspect that a floor is out of level or a wall is leaning.

A sagging ceiling may signify loose wallboard or plaster, and should be inspected more closely from the attic, if possible (see chapter 2). Bowed walls may indicate a weakness in the structural framework, consult with an inspector, engineer, or impartial contractor. Minor, localized sagging or softening of wall or ceiling materials may indicate a water leak above or behind the area in question. Water can travel along the house framework to areas surprisingly far from the point of entry; cracks in the roof can cause damage to ceilings and walls far away from the leak itself (see chapter 2). Also check for another common source of problems: loose, cracked, or missing caulking around bathtubs and shower stalls.

If you find a bowed area in a plaster ceiling and it sounds hollow when you tap it lightly, the area has probably pulled away from the lath backing. This situation is very common where wood lath strips were used. Some older wooden lathed homes have serious problems with failure of the ceiling plaster because these wood strips were placed too close together (see figure 6.4). If your attic is unfinished, look down at the wood lath of the ceiling below. If the wood strips are so close together that the ceiling plaster has not "curled," that is, squeezed up between the strips and hardened around them, the adhesion of the plaster has been compromised and this may be the cause of the sagging.

Cracks in Walls and Ceilings

Very fine, straight, generally parallel cracks in plaster walls and ceilings are of no great concern. Plaster has limited ability to flex with the structure of a home, and some cracks are inevitable. These kinds of cracks are common where gypsum lath was used. Typically 18 inches wide by 36 inches long, gypsum lathing was installed with butted joints and without any reinforcement across those joints. Cracking parallel to the joints is common and is repairable by coating the cracks with a flexible caulking and touching up with paint.

Cracks at angles opposed to each other and jagged, open cracks demand a closer look. If the cracks occur over a short period of time, look for the source. Poor drainage outside your home, or standing water underneath it, may be causing the soil to heave and shift the building. An improperly constructed foundation in a freezing climate could be another cause (see chapter 1).

Look closely with a magnifying glass at joints where two pieces of wallboard come together. Normally, these joints are covered with paper tape and layers of joint compound. If you find a crack at a joint, only cosmetic repairs are usually necessary, unless the crack gradually increases in size.

Cracks may change size from season to season as your home expands and contracts with the weather. Measure the size of any suspect, open cracks (greater than $\frac{1}{16}$ of an inch) and note the date. Cracks that grow larger should be carefully monitored. If the crack grows wider or if nearby doors and windows begin to jam, there's good reason to call in a professional to determine whether the cause of the problem is soil shifting underneath the house.

Minor hairline cracks occurring parallel to and about 1½ inches away from an outside corner on gypsum wallboards are usually caused by poorly installed corner reinforcements. This is easily corrected by securing the metal corner bead with more nails, applying joint compound over the area, and repainting.

Cracks in Floors

Cracks that appear in concrete slab floors or in rigid floor coverings such as ceramic tile or slate laid over a concrete slab should be closely analyzed. Trace the cracks to the outside wall where the face of the foundation is exposed. Here you can see if the crack runs up the wall or even through the foundation itself. Although hairline cracks are common

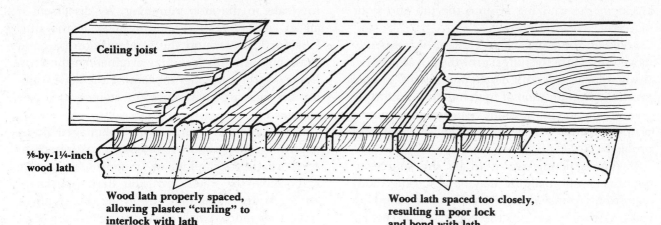

Ceiling joist

⅜-by-1¼-inch
wood lath

Wood lath properly spaced,
allowing plaster "curling" to
interlock with lath

Wood lath spaced too closely,
resulting in poor lock
and bond with lath

FIGURE 6.4 Section of a plaster ceiling

in any concrete structure, cracks wider than ⅛ inch or cracks that are out of vertical or horizontal alignment by more than ⅛ inch should be further analyzed by an inspector or engineer.

Floor Squeaks

Wood floors will rarely be squeak-free, in spite of the builder's best efforts. Since green, unseasoned lumber is commonly used in new construction, squeaks can occur later when the wood dries out. Squeaks are annoying, but are rarely a sign of structural problems. Squirting powdered graphite or talcum powder between the squeaking floorboards will often eliminate the noise for a time. More permanent solutions involve countersinking screws through the loose board and filling the hole with wood putty or, with floors on the first story where the subfloor is accessible from the basement, trying to secure the loose board by screwing into it from underneath.

Buckling Floors

Prolonged exposure to high humidity makes wood floors susceptible to buckling. A dehumidifier may

solve the problem temporarily; long-term solutions include better ventilation below the floor and in the attic, and better drainage around the home (see chapter 1).

Wood floors may also buckle if they have been installed without adequate expansion areas near adjoining rigid surfaces. Since wood expands and contracts with temperature changes, there must be sufficient space for expansion near walls, tiled floors, and other inflexible materials. Check with the manufacturer or supplier of your flooring regarding recommended gaps for expansion.

Odors and Fungal Growth

As you inspect your home, pay close attention to what your nose is telling you. A musty, damp, stale odor should be tracked to its source.

Check your crawl space or basement for moisture or damp soil, which may cause odors to enter the home (see chapters 1 and 2). Look and smell inside closets to determine whether they are adequately ventilated. Check laundry rooms, bathrooms, and kitchens for leaky pipes inside the walls or near the floors. Shower water in bathrooms is often continually splashed onto the floor, and, as mentioned, leaks down through any gaps or cracks in the caulking around the tub and floor material.

Look at the walls behind large, infrequently moved furniture for fungal growth such as mildew. It will appear as a dark blotch on the wall. Fungal growth is an indication of high indoor humidity or poor ventilation in the room. Sometimes, furniture placed too close to the wall surface will create the problem.

If the carpeting seems to be the source of odors, it or the padding may be absorbing moisture from ground water or from roof or plumbing leaks. Carefully pull up the corners of carpeting with pliers and inspect the backing and carpet padding for moisture and signs of rust and fungal growth. If the carpeting falls apart when you pull at it, you have a serious moisture problem in that area.

Areas most susceptible to musty odors and fungal growth are basements and rooms that are below the grade level. Below-grade rooms have interior floor levels lower than the outside grade of the soil. When moisture or staining is discovered on floors and along baseboards of these rooms, suspect water intrusion through the foundation slab, poor exterior drainage, or improper waterproofing of the foundation (see chapter 1).

Water Stains

Look carefully in each room, particularly around the baseboards and on the ceiling, for discoloration of the finishes. A water stain typically appears as a dark ring of discoloration around an affected area. Ceiling stains are not necessarily circular; water often runs along a ceiling joist and wallboard joint, resulting in long, narrow strips of discoloration.

Ceiling stains near or under a bathroom are most likely to have been caused by poor caulking, as mentioned, by a deteriorating seal at the toilet's floor gasket, or by bathtub or drain line overflow (see chapter 8). If there is no access to these areas, a professional builder may have to cut a small hole in the ceiling to find the source of the leak.

When a ceiling stain occurs below an attic, check for leaks in the attic plumbing. As discussed, if an air conditioner has been installed in the attic, look for leaks around the condensation pan and drain line. An attic leak may originate at the roof. Using a strong flashlight, examine the roof framing for signs of leaks above the stained area (see chapter 2).

Look for water stains around damaged floors near doors and windows. Cracked caulking, damaged weather stripping, or a poor seal may be responsible for water intrusion here (see chapter 5). Water stains may simply be the result of leaving a window partly open during a storm or of condensation dripping from glass or any metal trim. Condensation can be a particular problem in bathrooms and kitchens, which should be well ventilated.

Efflorescence

Moisture penetrating masonry or grouted tile can create a chalky white mineral deposit called efflorescence. Efflorescence is sometimes an early warning that excessive moisture is being absorbed into the concrete because of poor exterior drainage. Efflorescence can occur under resilient floor tiles or sheet flooring set on concrete floors, creating bumps and blisters. Correction might require any number of antimoisture remedies, such as improving foundation drainage, extending downspouts, or setting splash blocks so that water runs away from the affected area (see chapters 1 and 3).

Insect Damage

Look closely at exposed wood baseboards, trim, and door- and window jambs throughout the home for small tan or dark brown pellets or a sawdustlike material, indicating the presence of wood-destroying insects. Drywood termites shy away from light and will typically eat the interior portions of wood members and leave a thin skin of wood on the surface. The wood may open up eventually and release pellets onto the floor. Use a flashlight and

INTERIOR WALLS, CEILINGS, AND FLOORS

a scratch awl with a dull tip or other probe to determine the extent of the damage.

Another form of wood-destroying insect, the subterranean termite, invades wood by building tubelike mud tunnels upward from the soil (see chapter 1). The tunnels protect the insect from ants and light. Although they're usually spotted on foundations and in basements, the tunnels may also be found along baseboards, behind refrigerators, and inside cabinets. Termite infestation requires a professional exterminator.

Areas and Items Requiring Special Attention

A few areas of the house are particularly prone to damage or soiling, and some items require special attention to protect you and your family from hazards.

Bathrooms, Kitchens, and Laundry Rooms

Bathrooms, kitchens, and laundry rooms need extra attention because of the constant presence of moisture. Use a flashlight to check carefully inside cabinets—particularly under sinks—behind refrigerators, clothes washers, dishwashers, and around bathtubs and floors and walls for signs of water, mildew, or softening of surface materials. A sponginess or discoloration of the floor covering around the toilet could mean a leak in the seal where it connects to the floor. Look for damaged or missing caulking between the tubs, sinks, toilets, and the walls and floor. Joints between bathroom walls and sinks, bathtubs, or showers require caulking. It cannot be overemphasized that caulking is a simple and inexpensive method of moisture proofing that can save you hundreds or even thousands of dollars in later repairs.

Some tips follow that can help you do a neat, long-lasting caulk job in the bathroom:

- Clean the joints to be caulked with one-part household bleach to three-parts water.
- Cut the caulking tube's nozzle at a 45-degee angle.
- Hold the tube at that angle and *push* the nozzle along the joint as you squeeze compound into the joint.
- Dip an old butter knife in water and draw it along the joint to finish it off. Clean off excess caulk as instructed on the product label.

Check the dishwasher discharge pipe and the "air gap," a device that prevents waste water from being siphoned back into the dishwasher. It can clog and leak water (see chapter 8). The flexible hose connections on washing machines become brittle with age and should be replaced about every 3 to 5 years.

Kitchen cooking areas need inspection about once a month. Check your range ventilator hood for grease buildup and keep it clean. Light bulbs covered with grease should be cleaned or replaced. Inspect the hood's outside vent for an accumulation of grease. If you find a buildup, hire a professional to clean the ducts to avoid the risk of fire.

Stairways

Most home accidents involve a fall, and a full complement of these spills happen on the stairs. If your home has stairways, check the handrails for firmness. Make sure handrails extend fully from the bottom to the top of each stairway. The handrail should be easily gripped by a hand of average size; flat and wide designs do not permit a firm grasp. There should be at least a 1½-inch gap between the handrail and wall. Any balusters, which are the posts supporting the handrail, should be spaced so that a 6-inch sphere cannot pass through any portion. Check all the balusters for soundness as you go up the stairs.

Each step should have the same height (riser) and the same width (tread) to avoid constituting a tripping hazard. If the riser or the tread varies more than ⅜ inch from one step to another, or if the treads are less than 9 inches deep, consider remodeling the stairway; the significant hazard justifies the expense.

Fireplaces

Fireplaces should be inspected frequently. A smoky fireplace and excessive soot buildup are symptoms of poor "draw." As discussed in Chapter 3, look for tree limbs or other obstructions near the chimney top. In windy areas, a special wind cap may solve the problem of a smoky fireplace. In the worst case, you may need to have the chimney extended upward to increase its draw.

Carefully inspect the firebox, the area where the wood burns, to see if a heavy accumulation of soot or creosote has developed. Soot can decrease the draw of a fireplace significantly. Creosote is a shiny, black tarlike substance that can easily ignite and cause a chimney fire if allowed to accumulate. Removal of creosote is best done by a professional chimney sweep. Chimneys serving wood-burning stoves should be cleaned a minimum of once a year; if soft, resinous woods such as pine are burned, the chimney should be cleaned more often, at least twice at year. Chimneys serving open fireplaces should be inspected once a year and cleaned as needed or every 5 years. Burning well-seasoned hardwood such as oak or apple reduces the creosote and soot buildup.

Check the firebox for loose, cracked, or missing bricks. Cracks larger than ¼ inch and loose or damaged bricks should be repaired. These repairs require special heat-resistant materials and should be left to a qualified mason.

Many newer fireplaces, known as "pre-fab" or "zero-clearance" fireplaces, are manufactured and installed as a single preassembled unit. These units may have steel interiors or may be lined with masonry panels simulating brickwork. Expect minor cracking to occur in the simulated brick, but when areas behind the brick panels show excessive cracking, replacement of the unit is warranted. Excessive cracking shows that the integrity of the unit has been compromised.

Smoke Alarms

Test the operation of all smoke detectors at least once a month. Smoke detectors should be installed on hallway ceilings right outside each cluster of bedrooms, but no closer than 6 inches to a corner. Additional detectors should be placed in the basement, in the hallway of every floor, and in accessible attics. One additional detector should be placed inside the bedroom of any family member who smokes. Batteries should be replaced no less than once a year.

Maintenance Tips

Defects in ceilings, walls, and floors that are caused by more serious underlying problems simply don't come under the heading of routine maintenance and will require at least a consultation with an inspector, engineer, or other qualified professional. You can, however, successfully repair small cracks, caulk, paint, and clean. You'll probably be able to replace or install new resilient tiles. An ambitious and confident do-it-yourselfer may want to tackle resilient sheet flooring and wall-to-wall carpets. Leave sealing concrete slabs and cleaning chimneys to professionals.

Ceilings

Ceilings generally need little attention when properly constructed. The most common malady of painted or plaster ceilings is minor cracking. This is easily corrected with patching compound or flexible, paintable caulk; consult a home repair manual for techniques to patch various cracks.

Most homeowners can replace an acoustical ceiling tile or two, but ceilings sprayed with acoustical materials must be repaired by a professional contractor (although minor water stains can be masked with white shellac). *Caution:* Many acoustical materials installed before 1976 contain asbestos. Asbestos fibers can harm your health if inhaled, so never sand acoustical tiles containing asbestos, since this process can create airborne particles. Asbestos is considered a hazardous material requiring special techniques and equipment to contain or remove safely. If you suspect materials in your house contain asbestos, contact your local Environmental Protection Agency, listed in your telephone directory.

Don't be concerned about cracks running horizontally through a large ceiling beam or joist. This is a normal condition. But if the sight bothers you, such cracks can be covered up with wood filler. Cracks running perpendicular to the length of the beam, however, can be a serious problem. Consult a qualified professional for advice.

Walls

Wall damage is most commonly caused by simple physical abuse, as when furniture scuffs the wall or when a doorknob punches a hole in it. These two problems can easily be prevented. Chair-rail molding, installed about 2½ feet above the floor around the perimeter of a room, can protect walls from furniture; and doorstops, installed at the floor line, protect them from banging doors.

Ordinary nonabrasive household cleaning products are fine for cleaning walls. Ease of cleaning depends on the quality and kind of paint used initially. High-gloss and semi-gloss enamels clean more easily than paints with a flat finish. Treat mildew with one-part bleach to three-parts water and allow wet areas to dry thoroughly. Make certain any leaks have been corrected.

Structural problems affecting walls are uncommon. But when a problem is discovered, it is important to determine the cause, which may mean opening up the wall for inspection. Damaged wood studs or supports should be strengthened or replaced, another job for a professional builder.

Floors

Floors should be maintained by periodic cleaning and vacuuming. Regular, careful vacuuming can significantly extend the life of a carpet. For worn wood floors, try refinishing rather than entirely re-

surfacing: power buffing the floors with steel wool, wiping with mineral spirits, and applying another two to three coats of clear, penetrating sealer. Resurfacing involves time-consuming and tricky power sanding and requires considerable care. Most floors can be redone by simple refinishing.

Trouble-free floor coverings depend on good subflooring construction. Subfloors with too few or the wrong kind of nails will allow nails to pop up through resilient floors. Thin or otherwise inadequate subflooring can cause signifcant bowing of the floor. If you suspect a structural problem, call a professional to evaluate it.

Odors and Mildew

You can do a lot to control mildew and musty odors. Check all ventilating systems in the crawl space and attic (see chapters 2 and 3). Replace vent screens that have become clogged by debris or paint. Closets may become musty because of poor circulation; often the best solution is to install a ventilating fan or louvered doors to increase air circulation. Elevating closet doors about 1 inch above the floor to allow proper circulation may also do the trick.

Where mildew is found on walls behind furniture, provide additional space for air to circulate and repaint with a fungicidal additive in the paint. Install exhaust fans in the kitchen and bathrooms to reduce humidity; the fans must vent to the outside, not into the attic.

If your basement or crawl space has a dirt floor, try sealing the exposed earth with a sheet of plastic acting as a vapor barrier (see chapter 1). Often the soils beneath buildings appear to be relatively dry but contain considerable moisture.

Who Should Do the Work?

As discussed in this chapter, you can do much of the work on walls, ceilings, and floors by yourself. You can successfully repair small cracks, caulk, paint, and, of course, clean. In addition, you'll probably be able to replace or install new resilient tiles. An ambitious and confident do-it-yourselfer may even want to tackle resilient sheet flooring and wall-to-wall carpets.

But defects in walls, ceilings, and floors that are caused by more serious underlying problems will require at least a consultation with a professional. And sealing concrete slabs and cleaning chimneys are jobs best left to professionals.

Here, as with all home repairs, determining whether you should do the work yourself or hire a professional is a judgment call. Weigh your *honest* appraisal of your own expertise and time available for the project against the expense required to have someone else do the job for you. Reading Chapter 11 will help you make this determination.

PART II

Inside the Walls and Under the Floors

7

ELECTRICAL SYSTEM

Electricity found a place in our homes scarcely a century ago, and made itself indispensable almost immediately—for light, heat, and as the power source for many devices.

Telephones, door bells, intercoms, and most thermostat wiring operate at relatively harmless low voltage. But some of the electricity we use is potentially dangerous. Basic house wiring, called branch circuit wiring, can cause shock or fire if it has been installed incorrectly or has deteriorated. For this reason, it is advisable to maintain your electrical system in good order and to attend quickly to the necessary repairs.

Whatever advice on maintenance and repair is given here, it would be wise to have a licensed electrician do all but the simplest tasks. The operation of electrical devices is not always obvious, and even competent do-it-yourselfers and mechanically minded people should think twice before working with something as dangerous as electricity. Even if you protect yourself against shock and possible electrocution during a repair by turning the power off, you must eventually put the power back on. If the repair was improperly made, you risk power failure, fire, or worse from then on.

Before beginning the electrical inspection, it is a good idea to familiarize yourself with the basics of the system.

How the System Works

The electricity entering your home is called alternating current (AC) because it is created by large turbines and generators whose spinning coils and magnets reverse the flow of current periodically. Most household electronic devices require direct current (DC) and contain mechanisms that change the AC into DC. The force, or pressure, of the flow of electric current is measured in volts; the actual quantity of current that flows or is used is measured in amperes, or amps. Enough current or amperage, when given sufficient voltage, can do useful work in a given amount of time, which is the definition of *power*, measured in watts: amps × volts = watts.

Electricity from the utility company comes to your home by cables that either drop from an overhead pole or enter through an underground conduit. It passes through a meter, which records your power consumption. Electricity is delivered to your service panel, where it is broken into smaller branches. Breakers or fuses protect these branches against electrical short circuits or overload. The branch circuits run from the panel to the appliances, lighting, and outlets within the home.

The specifications for safe design of a system are laid out by the National Electrical Code®(NEC), which is revised periodically to include new standards. Local governments seldom require that older homes be updated to meet the code changes. If your home is more than 20 or 30 years old, its electrical system may not be fully adequate to meet today's power requirements. Don't take advantage of a "grandfather" loophole in local laws to get by with a substandard electrical system. If past owners have altered the system, hazards may exist that require correction.

Your inspection of your electrical system will be entirely visual; do not insert any probe or tool into any electrical panel or connection. Use a flashlight for dimly lit locations and a circuit analyzer, which is plugged into receptacles to verify that they are operating correctly. Circuit analyzers are available at most hardware stores. You will be looking to discover hazards that may exist and to estimate whether you have an adequate power supply for your needs.

The inspection should proceed in steps following the path through which electricity comes into the house: from the service entrance and main electrical panel, to the network of wires that provide electricity to the rooms, to the assortment of fixtures, appliances, outlets, and switches that are all dependent on electricity for their operation.

Service Entrance

Begin your inspection at the point where electrical power enters your home from the utility company's lines. With many newer homes, and some older ones, an underground conduit, or lateral, will bring the power cable to your meter. This conduit may be either metal or plastic pipe, usually about 2 inches in diameter. It should not be bent, broken, or open to water penetration. There is usually no problem with a lateral service, as long as excavation has not damaged it.

If you have an overhead cable drop, go outside to where it enters the home and look up at it. The typical overhead drop from a utility pole to a residence appears as three conductors loosely spiraled together, two of them insulated and one bare, shiny aluminum. Older installations may have two or three separate conductors, each one individually

supported. Where only two conductors are connected to the house, 120 volt power is available. If three conductors are observed, both 240 and 120 volt power will be available (see figure 7.1).

In the past, it was common for utility companies to supply voltage at approximately 110 and 220 volts. At present, most public utilities try to supply approximately 120 and 240 volt power for residential use. The actual voltage supplied to your home may still vary slightly from these values, but most home appliances are manufac-

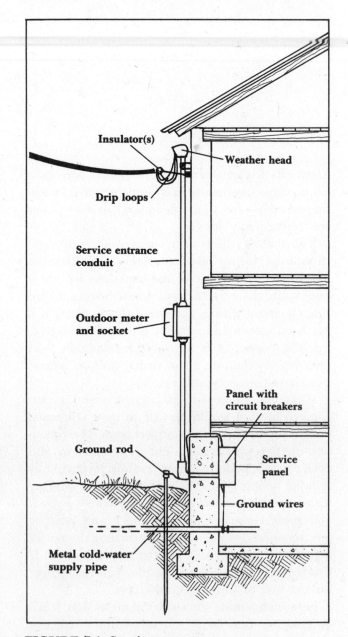

FIGURE 7.1 Service entrance

tured to tolerate slight variations of voltage without damage.

It is important for safety that the overhead drop clear the ground by at least 12 feet where vehicles may pass underneath and 10 feet above pedestrian traffic. It must also be at least 3 feet above any roof with a slope of less than 30 degrees, and it must not pass close to windows or anywhere else where a person could touch it. The drop must be free of vines, tree limbs, and other obstructions, and it must not be close enough to rub against them when the wind blows. If you see that the insulation is frayed or worn off any of the cables, you should inform the utility company.

The service drop must be properly supported where it reaches the house. Do *not* touch any of the electrical conductors. With older homes, the separate conductors are attached to insulators. In newer installations, the braided aluminum, neutral conductor may be used to support the weight of the power lines.

An overhead drop is generally spliced to the house entrance conductors in the air near the top of a service entrance cable, which is generally within a metal conduit. This conduit should be securely fastened to the house. It is topped by a weatherhead, facing down, into which the wires pass after forming a drip loop. The weatherhead and loop prevent rainwater from running down the service entrance cable. The entrance cable terminates in the meter housing. If the meter is on the outside of the house, it should also be securely fastened to the wall. If you believe that any part of this entry system is loose, or if you see frayed electrical cables or broken insulation, call your local electric utility company and ask for an inspector to examine the system.

The service equipment is usually located in a panel close to the meter (see figure 7.2). It normally consists of a metal box (weatherproof, if outside) and the following components: main disconnect device, overload protection (fuses or circuit breakers), and grounding wire. The main disconnect may be a switch or a pull out block with cartridge fuses. It is frequently labeled to indicate its capacity, and this is one way, although not a foolproof one, to determine the power available to the home. If the panel does not have a main disconnect, it should

take no more than six hand motions to disconnect all the power to the house; this requirement was established by the NEC for safety considerations in the event of a fire.

Check all circuit breakers by switching them off and on again. Since they are mechanical devices, circuit breakers may fail by not moving, by not disconnecting the power when switched off, or by not restoring power when switched back on. Have an assistant walk around the house to verify that

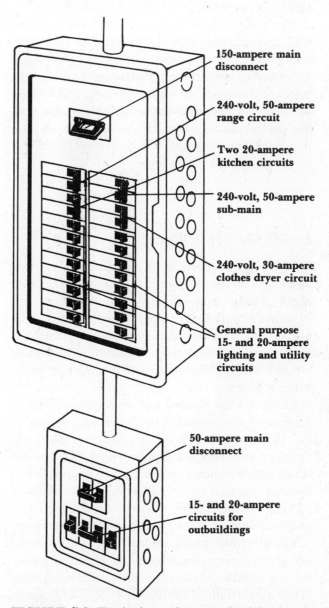

150-ampere main disconnect

240-volt, 50-ampere range circuit

Two 20-ampere kitchen circuits

240-volt, 50-ampere sub-main

240-volt, 30-ampere clothes dryer circuit

General purpose 15- and 20-ampere lighting and utility circuits

50-ampere main disconnect

15- and 20-ampere circuits for outbuildings

FIGURE 7.2 Typical service panel with circuit breakers

lights and appliances go off and on. Sometimes a circuit breaker will buzz or vibrate. Any of these indications require replacement of the breaker, which is a job only a licensed electrician should undertake.

Panel covers are provided with "knock-out" holes for wiring to pass through. Frequently, some of these have been removed and left uncovered; a careless person might put a finger or a tool through the resulting holes and into a live connection inside. Such holes should be covered with a spacer designed for the purpose—never with electrical tape.

The panel should be securely fastened to the wall, and no rust should be found in the panel enclosure. If you find any evidence of past water penetration, carefully seal the top and sides of the panel and around conduits entering and exiting the panel with exterior-grade caulking. If this does not correct the situation, the panel or its location may need to be changed. An electrician should re-secure any panel that is loose.

Inside the Main Panel

A thorough inspection of the electrical system would include the inside of the main circuit breaker panel. But because hazardous live terminals and wires are exposed when the protective inner cover of the panel is removed, only a qualified inspector or electrician should open this panel to inspect its interior wiring. Never take off the interior panel cover yourself.

An electrician can tell you whether the sizes of wires used are compatible with the fuses or break-ers. He or she can check that all connections are tight and that no insulation is melted or scorched, which would indicate an overload or arcing. Other hazards that may be found under the panel cover include double-tapping (more than a single wire under a bonding screw) and unprotected splices.

The electrical panels of many older homes do not provide enough amperage or electrical power for new appliances such as central air conditioning or for a modernized kitchen or a room addition to the home. Sometimes the capacity of the panel is sufficient in theory, but no actual space remains in the box itself for any additional circuit breakers and wiring. The electrician can tell you whether these conditions exist.

If you live in an older home with limited electrical capacity in the main panel, there's a chance that the previous owner created a serious hazard by trying to bypass the panel when altering the electrical system. Your own visual inspection of the system can help to discover such a situation. All power to lights and appliances within the home should pass through the fuses or breakers within the main electrical panel. If you disconnect all the main circuit breakers and fuses in this panel, no light fixture, appliance, or wall outlet in the home should operate. If you find otherwise, ask an electrician to investigate the situation. He or she may find, within the panel, an unfused circuit fed into the branch wiring directly from the main power line without passing through any overload protection—a serious fire hazard. This condition often indicates that the panel is no longer adequate for the power requirements of the home and needs upgrading.

Often more than one appliance is placed on a 240-volt circuit in a similar attempt to bypass a panel's power limitation. The NEC requires *each* 240-volt appliance to be on its own "dedicated" cir-cuit with a separate fuse or breaker. You can detect this hazard by counting the appliances in your home that use 240 volt power: the oven, range top, electric dryer, electric water heater, central air con-ditioner, and electric furnace. You should have the same number of 240-volt circuit breakers or fuse blocks in the main panel. Each circuit breaker or fuse should disconnect just one of these major ap-pliances. Another clue to the existence of this haz-ard is an illegal cable running behind cabinets from one heavy appliance receptacle to another. If you suspect either of these conditions, call an electrician to investigate the situation.

If your home contains a fuse box with the old "Edison" screw-in fuses, an electrician should check their capacity. As a rule, the older branch circuits are wired with Number 14-gauge conductor and should be protected by fuses with a 15-amp rating. (Main fuses may be as high as 30 amps.) It's all too common, however, to discover 20- or 30-amp fuses in place of the 15-amp fuses. Someone has inserted higher-amperage fuses to use more appliances than the circuit was designed to serve. This is a serious hazard, because larger fuses allow too much current to pass through the wires, which can lead to overheating and fire. *Never* replace fuses with ones with a higher rating.

You may choose to use "type S" (tamper-proof) fuses of appropriate rating. (*Note:* Type S fuses are not available in Canada.) This fuse employs an adapter that, once inserted into the receptacle, cannot be removed and will allow fuses to be changed but will not permit fuses of a higher rating to be installed. All type S fuses now made are time-delay fuses, which will allow a larger current to flow through the circuit briefly without blowing. This time delay allows motorized appliances such as refrigerators and washing machines to draw a heavy load for a second or two when starting up, but does not permit a continuous overload that would overheat the wiring. The type S fuse may solve some overload problems, but if not, the size of the main electrical panel may have to be increased and new circuits added, which is a job for an electrician.

In many installations the cables will be concealed where they leave the panel. But if they are visible, look for metal conduit and nonmetallic sheathed cable to be protected by bushings where they pass through the side of the panel (see figure 7.3). A bushing is a sleeve fitted into the opening of a junction box to protect wires from abrasion. If you find any cables or conduit pasing through the side of the panel without bushings, your electrician should make a repair. The ground wire, however, requires no bushing.

The Ground Wire

Your inspection should also include a check for grounding. The main electrical panel must be grounded to a rod driven into the earth or attached to a metal cold-water supply pipe. Homes built or rewired since 1978 are required to have *both* of these ground connections (only one is required in Canada). Grounding reduces the chances of shock, fire, or damage to appliances and motors, and helps protect the home from lightning. Grounding permits stationary appliances such as washing

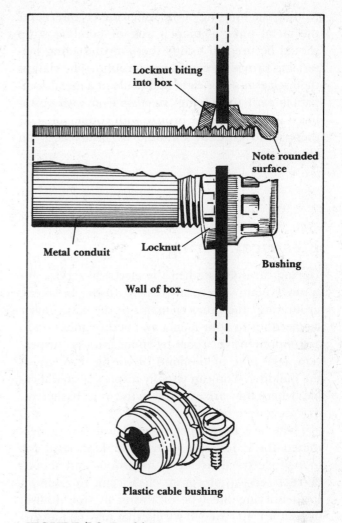

Locknut biting into box

Note rounded surface

Metal conduit

Locknut

Bushing

Wall of box

Plastic cable bushing

FIGURE 7.3 Bushings

machines, clothes dryers, refrigerators, ranges, microwave ovens, as well as computers and certain power tools, to be used safely.

The ground wire from the panel is commonly a bare copper or aluminum wire, Number 6 gauge (about the diameter of a common pencil) or larger. It may be found running from the panel (as mentioned, no bushing is required here) through the basement wall and to a clamp fastened around the stub of a grounding rod driven into the earth. The clamp should be secure and the grounding wire unbroken and out of the way of foot traffic. The ground wire should never be spliced.

Where the ground wire is clamped to a water pipe, you should trace the pipe from that point until it enters the earth at the side wall of the foundation. If any nonconducting plastic piping, including the housing of the water meter, interrupts the metal pipe, a jumper wire or bonding strap should be used to bridge the nonconducting material to provide a continuous ground. The clamps themselves must be tight and made of a metal compatible with the piping: steel or iron with galvanized iron; copper or bronze with copper pipe. If there is no ground, it should be installed by an electrician.

Electrical Wiring

Having carefully studied the electrical service entrance, main electrical panel, fuses, breakers, grounding, and other elements of the basic power connections to your home, and before going on to a comprehensive, room-by-room interior inspection, take note of the kind of wiring throughout the building. You can visually inspect electrical cables where they are exposed in the attic, basement, or garage (see figure 7.4).

There are four types of electrical wiring permitted for indoor use. Any other kind used for branch electrical circuits is hazardous and should be replaced—a job for an electrician. In addition to identifying the type of wiring in your house, inspect for jury-rigged wiring that may be hazardous. One giveaway here is the existence of lamp cord spliced into wall receptacles, ceiling fixtures, and junction boxes. Also look for exposed electrical connections, those that are not contained within junction boxes. Neither taped wire splices nor splices made with plastic wire nuts should be found outside these boxes, which must be fitted with covers. The only exceptions are the original connections of knob-and-tube wiring (see below), which are soldered and taped.

The earliest electrical installations in homes commonly used knob-and-tube wiring (see figure 7.5). This type of wiring, with its original soldered and taped connections, may be safe if it is not buried in insulation and if it does not run exposed along the walls or ceilings of any living area. A hazard with this old wiring, however, is that past owners may have spliced into it in an improper manner or

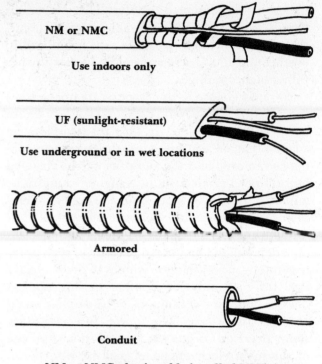

NM or NMC

Use indoors only

UF (sunlight-resistant)

Use underground or in wet locations

Armored

Conduit

NM or NMC plastic cable is called NMD in Canada. UF plastic cable is called NMW.

FIGURE 7.4 Types of wire

overloaded individual circuits by adding outlets "down the line." A hazard also exists where wire insulation is cracked or missing.

Nonmetallic sheathed cable, abbreviated "NM" or "NMC" and often called simply Romex, a brand name, appeared for use in homes in the 1930s. Typically it is concealed within the walls of a home. It should not be exposed in the basement or any living area, but it may be buried beneath insulation in an attic provided that it is securely fastened to the attic joists.

Strands of insulated wires are drawn through metal conduits, typically made of steel and hand-shaped to turn corners and avoid obstacles. Some types of conduit are threaded together, but most are joined by bushings to other lengths of conduit and to junction boxes. You may find metal conduit in interior or exterior use. You should never see the individual wires themselves.

Older homes may have some armored cable, or "BX" cable, a spiral-wound, galvanized-steel, flex-

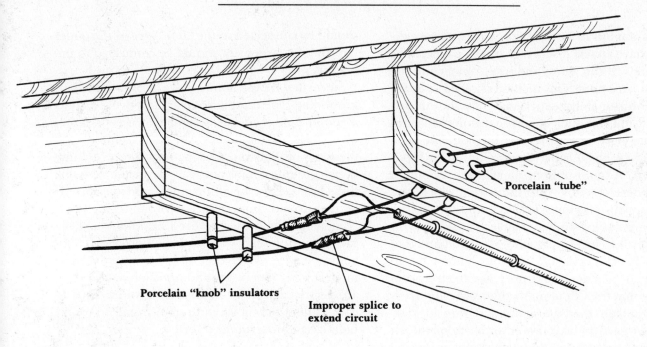

FIGURE 7.5 Knob-and-tube wiring

ible conduit that carries wires inside. It is joined with bushings.

All outdoor wiring must be run through rigid metal conduit or use UF (sunlight-resistant) cable, which is tough and weatherproof. Check the cable where it enters the building, and read the markings on the plastic. The cable should be clearly marked "UF." All outdoor fittings and receptacles should be weatherproof. Where ordinary nonmetallic cable is used outside or buried underground, it should be replaced; call in a qualified electrician to do the job.

Aluminum Wiring

Aluminum wiring was used widely in residential construction between 1965 and 1976. Solid aluminum wire can be hazardous in the branch circuit wiring of a home. If any part of your wiring was installed during these years, you should inspect to see whether it is aluminum. Aluminum has a silver color throughout, and should not be confused with tinned copper wire. You will be able to read the printed label on plastic sheathed cable where it is exposed in unfinished areas such as the garage, attic, and basement. Aluminum wire can be identified by the markings, "AL," "ALUM," or "ALUMINUM." An electrician can also see the exposed ends of the conductors when he or she removes the inner protective cover of the main panel.

Most problems have arisen with solid aluminum wire, size Number 10 and Number 12 gauge, which was commonly used for utility and lighting circuits. The problem concerns the cut ends, or terminations, of the aluminum wire where they are connected under copper bonding screws or with wire nuts to circuit breakers, outlets, switches, or to other wires. The bonding screws and wire nuts do not always hold the aluminum securely. The copper and aluminum expand and contract at different rates, which sometimes causes the connections to loosen. The result is sparking, oxidation, greater heat, further loosening, and perhaps a fire. Although the early hardware, marked CU-AL, was designed for aluminum, it didn't always work; subsequent, heavier hardware, marked "CO/ALR," didn't work much better. Faced with liability suits, the electrical industry stopped using aluminum wire in branch circuits.

In an attempt to head off problems, some electricians have attached short lengths of copper wire at the ends of the aluminum wire, connecting the two with wire nuts. This method is called "pigtailing." Unfortunately, experience has shown that the wire nuts of such pigtailed connections can overheat. Only one corrective method has been approved by the United States Consumer Product Safety Administration, namely the Copulum method developed by Amp Industries, which uses a high-pressure bonding tool to crimp the copper and aluminum together in a molecular bond. This method looks a lot like pigtailing, so if you find that the aluminum terminations in your home have already been "pigtailed" to copper, ask an electrician to verify that the Copulum method was employed.

It is unlikely that the aluminum wire in your home will need to be removed or abandoned. An electrician can redo all the connections using the Copulum splices and copper wire. Some electricians will simply apply antioxidant and tighten all connections. This makes the wiring safe—temporarily. But all connections must be retightened every year, so more permanent repair is highly recommended.

Room-by-Room Inspection

Now you can begin to inspect the condition of your electrical outlets, wall switches, and light fixtures. The standard 15-amp, 120-volt outlets used until 1960 in the United States and Canada had two identical slots into which the plug of a lamp or appliance could be inserted. Now the slots are of different sizes, as are the metal prongs on the plugs of many devices that require correct polarity. Enforcing the plug orientation by using these different-size slots and prongs is an effort to maintain polarity, to ensure that one side of the appliance—usually a vulnerable element—is connected to the neutral side of the circuit. For many lamps, toasters, and simple home appliances, polarity is not important. Some sophisticated home appliances, especially those that use microcomputers, will operate more reliably if correct polarity is maintained. To ensure that polarity is correct, the smaller slot

should be connected to the "hot" wire in the outlet box and the larger slot should be connected to the neutral wire.

Since the 1960s, homes have been wired with grounding-type receptacles that have two slots plus a round hole, and are designed to accept three-wire plugs. Older homes can be retrofitted with these grounding receptacles only where a functional ground connection can be made. Usually, these homes have metallic conduit, and at each outlet the ground connection is wired to the conduit. Nonmetallic cable used before 1960 did not usually carry a grounding wire, and neither does knob-and-tube wire, so neither of these can easily be modernized. Where grounding is necessary, have an electrician run an individual ground wire to each outlet where it is required or install a ground fault circuit interrupter (GFCI).

Outlets

The GFCI protects people from severe electric shock by monitoring the current and disconnecting the circuit if it senses a current imbalance, indicating a diversion of electric current to ground, possibly through a human body. In that event, the GFCI acts like a small circuit breaker. The NEC requires GFCIs for outdoor receptacles, bathroom and garage receptacles, and at least one basement receptacle, as well as for those above the countertop within 6 feet of the kitchen sink. A GFCI looks much like an ordinary duplex wall outlet, with the addition of a pair of small buttons in the center. These buttons may be marked "test" and "reset" or simply "T" and "R."

Test the GFCI monthly by pressing the test button and resetting it. If it does not reset, the outlet should be replaced. Replacing a GFCI receptacle is more complicated than replacing an ordinary one and is best left to an electrician.

Here's how to test for correct polarity, grounding, and how to tell a live from a dead outlet. You will need a three-prong circuit tester, which can be purchased for between five and ten dollars at most hardware stores. If your home is equipped with modern, grounded outlets with three holes, this device will quickly and easily allow you to determine whether the outlets are energized and correctly wired for polarity and ground. Go through the rooms of the house inserting the tester into each receptacle and make a note wherever you find conditions that need to be corrected. It's handy to use adhesive-backed colored labels to identify faulty receptacles for the electrician.

If you have the older two-hole receptacles, you must also purchase an adapter that will fit onto your three-prong tester and plug into your receptacles. Get the adapter with the little green tab, not the one with the green wire. When you plug your tester into the outlets, push the green tab against the screw in the center of your receptacle cover plate. Your tester will indicate whether the polarity is correct and whether the screw is connected to a ground wire, which would permit the installation of three-prong receptacles.

The outlets themselves should be conveniently located so that you don't have to use extension cords or multiplier plugs. Modern code specifies that no point on any wall should be more than 6 feet from an outlet. In many older homes, it was considered sufficient to have only two outlets per room. This is likely to be inadequate for the homes of today.

In bedrooms and occasionally in living and dining rooms it's common for electrical outlets to be controlled by wall switches, so that lamps can be turned on and off from the doorway. Don't give up on a receptacle that tests as "dead" until you've turned on the wall switches.

Receptacles should be in good physical condition. Mark for replacement any that are painted over, scorched, cracked, broken, or that don't hold a plug securely. Where you find a rusted receptacle, for example, in a damp basement wall, the entire receptacle box may need to be replaced and carefully waterproofed. Loose outlets should be tightened to the box holding them, and where boxes themselves are loose, they too should be fastened securely. Record these conditions for your electrician.

Switches and Lamps

As you pass through each room, also direct your attention to wall switches and lamps. In old houses, light fixtures hanging on cords from the ceiling should be replaced because the wire insulation may be damaged. Wherever wires are exposed on old fixtures, look for frayed insulation. Point it out to your electrician as a hazard requiring new wiring.

Old push button and toggle switches may be inoperable and should be marked for replacement. Test all switches for proper function. Any switch that sparks, double clicks, or works only when pushed to the end of its throw will need to be replaced. Switches that feel warm or hot should also be replaced.

Three- and four-way switches make it possible to turn lights on and off from more than one location. Do-it-yourselfers frequently wire these incorrectly when replacing switches, with the result that a hall light, for example, can be turned off by one switch but only turned on again by another switch. Such a condition calls for the attention of an electrician.

A few homes are equipped with a low-voltage switching system for the lights, in which a series of switches electrically activate a set of relays located in the attic or some other concealed location. The advantage of this system is that you can control lighting in a remote part of the house from a central location such as the master bedroom. The disadvantage is that the relays may require replacement, and they can be hard to find. This too is a job for an electrician.

During your inspection of the light fixtures, turn off the light switch, remove any decorative globes that enclose light bulbs, and inspect for "overlamping." The permissible wattage is usually stamped somewhere on the body of the fixture. Remove any bulbs of greater wattage than the fixture is designed to accommodate. Using a higher wattage bulb may cause heat to build up in the fixture, weakening the insulation on the wiring inside the fixture and possibly causing a fire. Where you find melted shades, scorching, or heat discoloration, point the condition out to your electrician and ask whether the fixture needs replacement.

Recessed light fixtures in the ceiling may also overheat if they protrude into the attic and insulation has been packed around them (see chapter 2). If you haven't already done an attic inspection, go into your attic and check. (Follow the instructions and precautions given in chapter 2.) A properly installed recessed lighting fixture will be surrounded by a sheet metal or wire cylinder that is vented to allow heat to escape. If this is absent, you can make such a cylinder yourself. Disconnect the power to the light at the fuse or breaker, pull the insulation back from the fixture, and install the cylinder. Repack the insulation so that it does not cover the vent at the top.

Special Hazards

Extension cords can be a hazard. If you have to use them, your home probably requires additional electrical outlets. They should never be secured with nails or staples, run through walls, under doors, or under carpets. These situations pose shock and fire hazards. Note that the wire gauge of an extension cord should never be thinner than the cord of the appliance it serves.

Appliance and lamp cords must not have frayed or damaged insulation, and there must always be a cover over the wire connections in the plug. Never pull a plug out of a receptacle by the wire; always pull by the plug itself.

Although no home should be without smoke detectors in good working order, you shouldn't rely on them exclusively. Take an active role in fire prevention in your home by looking out for the following indications of electrical overheating: warm electrical cover plates; smoke or sparks at switches or outlets; the smell of burning plastic at switches or outlets; flickering lights; or wall outlets or entire circuits that won't work. Disconnect the power at the circuit breaker or fuse and call an electrician at once if you find any one of these conditions.

Estimating Your Requirements

Making a map of the circuits in your home will help identify insufficiencies in your system. Once you have determined that all the outlets are functional, disconnect one circuit at a time and make a list or diagram of all the outlets and fixtures served by that circuit. Number each circuit breaker or fuse in your main panel. Have a helper turn each one off, one after another, while you, using your tester, list every receptacle and light that is inoperative at that moment. For example, for the house shown in Figure 7.6, the list should read as follows:

Circuit 1. Master bedroom and bath, outlets and lights.

Circuit 2. Two upstairs bedrooms, outlets and lights.

Circuit 3. Living- and dining-room outlets; kitchen lights.

Circuit 4. Lavatory.

Circuit 5 and 6. Kitchen appliances.

Circuit 7. Electric range.

Circuit 8. Clothes dryer.

Circuit 9. Washing machine.

Circuit 10. Furnace motor.

Circuit 11. Basement lights and outlets.

Next add up the watts consumed by all the fixtures, appliances, and light bulbs on each circuit. Look for the wattage on the manufacturer's rating plate of each appliance, or you can approximate by using Table 7.1. The maximum allowed wattage for a 15-amp circuit at 120 volts is 1,500; on a 20-amp circuit it is 2,000 watts. As mentioned, certain appliances should have a dedicated 240-volt circuit (see page 74). Modern code also requires a separate circuit for each stationary appliance, as follows: furnaces, dishwashers, refrigerators, disposals, air conditioners, microwave ovens, whirlpools, well and septic pumps, GFCI circuits, and every electric baseboard heater. If you find that your home has one or more circuits that are overloaded, consider hiring an electrician to install additional circuits.

If your main electrical panel has no room for expansion, you will need to install a new panel with a higher rating. Almost every home today requires at least 100 amps at 120/240 volts at the main panel. Homes with central air conditioning, an electric clothes dryer, and an electric range may require 150 amps. Electric heat, in addition, may require 200 amps.

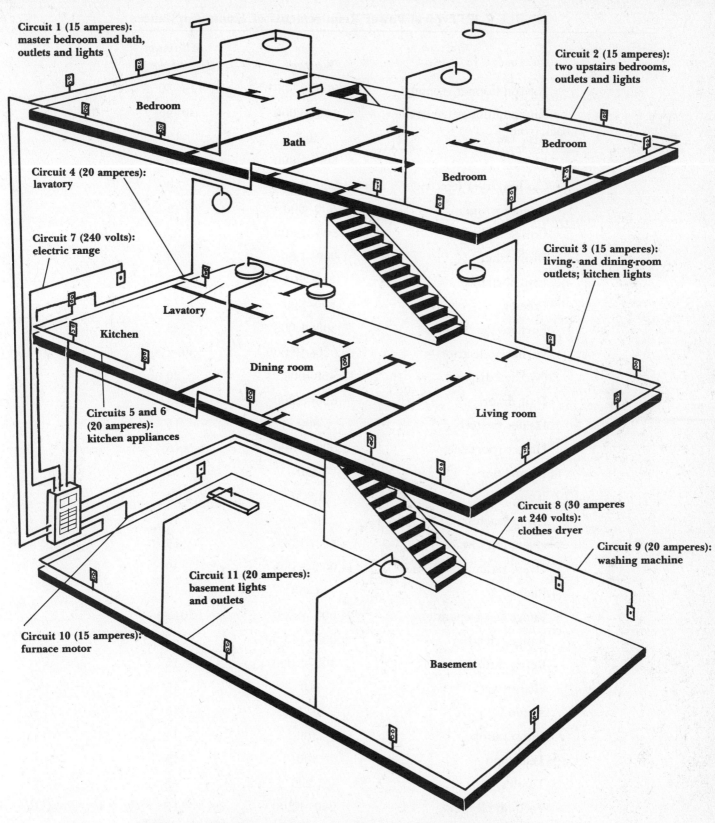

Circuit 1 (15 amperes):
master bedroom and bath,
outlets and lights

Circuit 2 (15 amperes):
two upstairs bedrooms,
outlets and lights

Circuit 4 (20 amperes):
lavatory

Circuit 7 (240 volts):
electric range

Circuit 3 (15 amperes):
living- and dining-room
outlets; kitchen lights

Circuits 5 and 6
(20 amperes):
kitchen appliances

Circuit 8 (30 amperes
at 240 volts):
clothes dryer

Circuit 9 (20 amperes):
washing machine

Circuit 11 (20 amperes):
basement lights
and outlets

Circuit 10 (15 amperes):
furnace motor

Bedroom

Bath

Bedroom

Bedroom

Lavatory

Kitchen

Dining room

Living room

Basement

Ideally, not all outlets and lights on a floor are on the same circuit; if
a fuse or circuit breaker blows, some of the rooms will still have light.

FIGURE 7.6 Typical circuit map

TABLE 7.1 Typical Power Requirements of Home Appliances

	Wattage	Minimum Circuit Amps
Air conditioner (room)	800–2,500	15–30
Air conditioner (central)	2,500–6,000	30–40
Attic fan	400	15
Blender	500–1,000	15
Clothes dryer (electric)	4,000–6,000	30
Clothes washer	500–800	15
Coffee maker	500–1,000	20
Dishwasher	1,000–1,800	20
Fan, portable	50–200	15
Freezer	300–500	15
Furnace (gas or oil)	300–1,000	15
Furnace (electric)	9,000–19,000	50–100
Garbage disposal	450–900	20
Hair dryer	600–1,200	15
Heater (waterbed)	800	15
Heater (portable)	1,000–1,500	15
Humidifier	450	15
Iron	1,000	15
Lamp (each bulb)	25–250	15
Oven, microwave	500–1,000	15
Oven, radiant (separate)	4,000–5,000	30
Radio	4–50	15
Range top (separate)	4,000–8,000	30–40
Range (electric)	8,000–14,000	50–70
Refrigerator	400–1,000	15
Shaver	10	15
Stereo	50–300	15
Sump pump	300	15
Television	300	15
Toaster	1,200	15
Vacuum cleaner	250–1,200	15
Water heater (electric)	4,500	30

Note: Actual wattage should be verified by checking the rating plate on each appliance.

Light Maintenance Duties

In contrast to other systems of your home, the electrical system requires little routine maintenance. Once you've made a thorough inspection and improved the system as necessary, you have little to worry about.

Where your overhead service drop passes close to tree limbs, check from time to time to make sure that they have not grown close to the cable. It's especially important to inspect for this condition if your area gets heavy snowfall. Pruning tree limbs in the vicinity of overhead electrical lines can be extremely hazardous and should be left to professionals. In many locations, the public utility company is responsible for the condition of the lines to your meter and its staff will undertake this task on request.

If the branch circuits of your home are wired with aluminum, have an electrician come every year or so to inspect for loose connections and to tighten them. If the terminations have been properly upgraded with Copulum connectors, this should not be necessary.

Some electricians recommend "exercising" all circuit breakers once a year by flipping them off and on again by hand to make sure that they will trip when required.

Special Problems

Overloaded circuits are often indicated by flickering or dimming lights when appliances are turned on and by frequently blowing fuses or tripping circuit breakers. In some cases, appliances will not operate at full power and the TV image will shrink when another appliance is turned on. On the other hand, if all the lights in your house flicker intermittently and appliances are *not* running, your system ground may be inadequate or loose. This problem is rare in houses but sometimes is found in mobile homes.

Overload or Short Circuit?

It is important to distinguish between an overload and a short circuit when a fuse or breaker opens. In an Edison fuse, an overload typically melts the element, whereas a short circuit blackens the glass. For other fuses and circuit breakers, follow these steps to track down the cause of the problem:

Turn off all switches and unplug all lamps and appliances on the affected circuit. Then install a new fuse or reset the tripped breaker. If the fuse blows or the breaker trips right away, it's likely that you have a short in a switch or receptacle. Disconnect power to the circuit. Carefully remove the cover plates of switches and outlets on this circuit and use a flashlight to inspect them for charred wire insulation, melted wires, or scorch marks. Never touch or probe inside the outlet or switch box. Replace defective switches or outlets yourself *only* if you are experienced in this kind of work and take all necessary safety precautions, especially turning off the affected circuit at the main panel. Otherwise, call an electrician. Always use a qualified professional electrican to replace defective wiring.

If the fuse or breaker does not disconnect the circuit again immediately when you replace or trip it, turn on the wall switches one at a time. If turning on a switch causes the short, inspect the switch, fixture, or outlet controlled by that switch.

If none of the switches has caused the circuit to disconnect, check each lamp or appliance by reconnecting them one at a time. If each one can be individually connected and turned on, the problem is likely to have been an overload caused by the use of all the appliances and lamps on the circuit at the same time. Carry out wattage calculations described earlier to determine whether an overload exists.

You may balance the load of your system by plugging some of the appliances or lamps into outlets served by another circuit, if you can do this *without* using extension cords. If this creates an overload on the second circuit, your wiring may be inadequate.

Occasionally a refrigerator or other motor-driven appliance will draw far too much power on starting up, causing an overload on the circuit. If one particular appliance appears to be the culprit, have it checked by a repair person.

High Electric Bills

Excessive consumption of electrical power in a home usually signals itself by higher-than-average utility bills. If your home is heated by electrical resistance heat or a heat pump, see the sections in this book on the heating system, insulation, and weatherproofing. If you live in a gas- or oil-heated home and you believe that your electric bill is higher than it should be, ask the utility company for the records of comparable, neighboring homes equipped with similar types of appliances. If this evidence suggests that your home consumes substantially more electrical power than average, analyze carefully whether you are using electrical heating appliances more than necessary. Room heating with space heaters, for example, is an impractical way to supplement the central heating sys-

tem, unless it too is an electrical resistance unit. Eliminate electric space heating, and recheck your power consumption.

If consumption remains high, have the utility company check your meter. In addition, follow the company's advice for reducing your power consumption—an inefficient refrigerator is one common culprit, overuse of air conditioning another. You may want to look over bills for a year or two back to see if you can identify a point when the bill went up dramatically. This may give you a clue about what appliance or change in habits has caused greater consumption.

Thus, with some detective work, you can discover the cause or causes of unusually high electric bills and take the steps necessary to bring them in line with the norm for comparable houses.

8

PLUMBING

Modern plumbing systems have made our lives more convenient and healthier. But if improperly maintained, even today's reliable systems can fail. Fortunately, most plumbing problems can be avoided if the homeowner has a basic understanding of how the system operates, and practices a little preventive maintenance.

The interior plumbing system is, in reality, three distinct systems: a water supply system, a drain-waste system, and a vent system—all of which will be covered at length in this chapter. But first a few words about your water source are in order.

Your Water Source

If water is supplied by a utility company, your responsibility is normally limited to maintaining the water-service line on your property. However, the point at which responsibility begins varies greatly, depending on the community. For example, sometimes the homeowner must maintain the service line starting at the water main rather than the property line. Check with your local water utility to find out where your responsibility lies.

If your water is supplied by a well, the well will fall under one of two classifications according to its depth: shallow (depths of 25 feet to 50 feet or less) and deep (50 feet or more). Water is pumped out of the well by a motorized pump, into a pressure tank, and into the house. The pump is controlled by a pressure switch which usually operates at between 20 to 40 or 30 to 50 pounds per square inch (psi). When demand in the house causes pressure in the tank to drop to the lower reading, the pump turns on and water is drawn out of the well to refill the pressure tank. The pump shuts off when the upper pressure limit is reached. The tank is partly filled with air to allow water to flow to the house.

There are three different types of pumps: submersible pumps, jet pumps, and piston pumps. Submersible pumps are used mostly for deep wells and are located within the well casing. The pump, motor, and wiring are designed to be submerged in water and push water up to the pressure tank. This pump is virtually maintenance-free, but if repairs are necessary the pump has to be removed from the well.

Jet pumps are used for both shallow and deep wells. With shallow wells, the centrifugal pump and jet assembly are located above the well head. With deep wells, the jet assembly may be in the well.

Piston pumps are found in older well installations and can be used for either deep or shallow wells. With deep wells, the piston assembly is located within the well, and the motor is aboveground. A shallow-well piston assembly and motor are both located above the well. Both types are powered by a pulley and belt connected to the motor.

Water Supply System

Potable water, supplied by a utility company or private well, flows into most homes at a pressure of 20 to 80 pounds per square inch through a water-service line whose diameter varies from ¾ to 1 inch (see figure 8.1). (*Note:* Plumbing pipe sizes refer to inside diameters rather than outside diameters.) A main shut-off valve is usually installed on the line near where it enters the building. Once inside the house, the pipe size is usually ½ to ¾ inch in diameter where it is connected to the water softener or water heater. From the water heater, the piping branches out horizontally and vertically in risers, typically ½ inch in diameter, to fixtures such as tubs, showers, and sinks.

Ideally, horizontal pipes should be installed with a slight pitch so that the entire system can be drained through a valve at its lowest point. The ability to drain the entire water supply system is important to facilitate repairs (or to prevent the pipes from freezing if the house is left vacant and must be completely winterized).

Supply piping should have another feature: air chambers. When water faucets are rapidly shut off, the resulting abrupt halt of water flow can cause pipes to bang, or "hammer." The enormous pressure created by this water hammer can even rupture the piping system. To prevent water hammering, capped-off sections of air-filled pipe (called air chambers) or commercially manufactured shock absorbers are installed on both hot and cold water pipes near each faucet to absorb the shock of this sudden change in water flow (see figure 8.2).

We expect a reasonable amount of water to flow out of faucets. Trying to take a shower or water the lawn with low water flow can be very annoying and inconvenient. Poor water flow is most often caused by corrosion or mineral buildup inside the water supply pipes and not necessarily by low pressure. Even when water pressure is in the normal range, water flow can be diminished if the interior diameter of a pipe has been reduced by corrosion or mineral deposits. Water flow is judged to be sufficient by most home inspectors when the water coming from an upper-story bathroom sink faucet, for example, is not significantly reduced when the bathtub faucet is left open at the same time.

Water Supply Piping

Most interior residential water supply systems use one of the following materials for piping: galvanized iron, copper, brass, or plastic. Sometimes more than one pipe material is used. Regardless of the material used, all piping systems must be adequately supported by or attached to the studs or joists with compatible wire hangers, clamps, or other approved devices.

Lead pipes were sometimes used for the main water supply line in older homes. Scratching the surface of lead pipe will reveal a dull gray color, and the connections are spherical or onionlike bulges. Because of the risk of elevated lead levels, you should have such pipes replaced. At the very least, have a laboratory test your water for lead content.

Copper tubing is similar in color to a penny and is available in soft, flexible, or rigid forms. It can last a very long time, except in areas of highly acidic water, where it can corrode. Copper tubing can be joined by soldered, compression, or flared (for soft tubing only) fittings. Solder is silver colored and is available in amalgams of 50 percent tin to lead down to 95 percent tin to 5 percent lead, or 95 percent tin to antimony (95/5). Amalgams containing more than 5 percent lead were banned for use in plumbing in 1984.

The hazards of lead contamination in your water supply cannot be overemphasized. Even with only short-term exposure, too much lead in the human body can damage the brain, nervous system, kidneys, and blood. Children and pregnant women are at greatest risk. Tissue damage from lead poisoning may be irreversible. If you have "soft," slightly acidic water or a system design where water can sit in pipes undrained for several hours, or

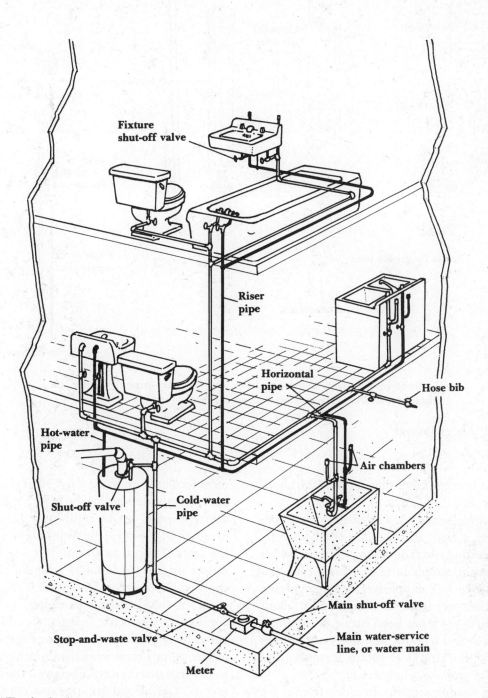

FIGURE 8.1 Typical water supply system

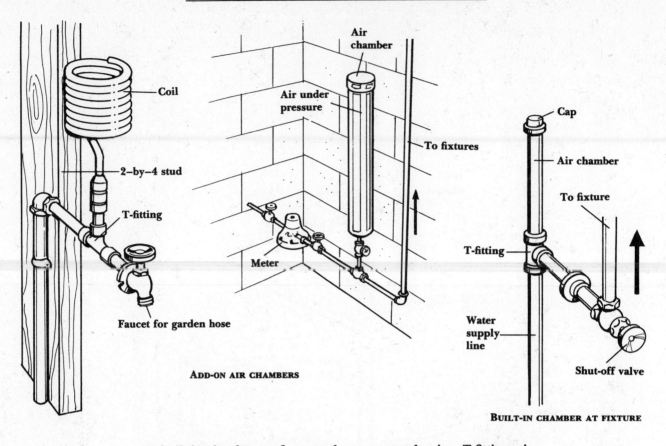

Coil

2–by–4 stud

T-fitting

Faucet for garden hose

Air chamber

Air under pressure

To fixtures

Meter

ADD-ON AIR CHAMBERS

Cap

Air chamber

To fixture

T-fitting

Water supply line

Shut-off valve

BUILT-IN CHAMBER AT FIXTURE

In built-in chambers at fixtures, the water supply pipe, T-fitting, air chamber, and cap are hidden behind the wall.

FIGURE 8.2 Air chambers

simply if your home is more than 5 years old, check the water for lead.

Have a sample tested by a laboratory that specializes in water analysis. Since lab results can be uneven, submitting two samples might be the wisest course. Replacing supply lines or adding filtration devices are sure but expensive solutions to the problem. At the very least, let water run for about 3 minutes whenever it has been sitting in the pipes for more than several hours, and don't use hot tap water to make hot drinks or infant formula (lead dissolves more readily in hot water).

Galvanized iron piping and threaded fittings are silver-gray and easily identified by their magnetic property. Galvanized piping is especially susceptible to decay caused by chemical action or by a decrease in its inner diameter caused by mineral buildup. As a result, its average life expectancy in

most locales is no more than 30 years, but this can vary greatly depending on water quality. Copper tubing should not be connected directly to galvanized piping because the contact between water and the ferrous (iron) and nonferrous (copper) metals causes an electrochemical reaction that corrodes the metals and eventually causes leaks. To properly separate these dissimilar metals, nonconducting connectors (dielectric unions) should be installed between galvanized and copper water lines. Dielectric unions have insulating washers and sleeves to prevent direct contact between the incompatible metals. Galvanized piping also contains a small amount of lead in the galvanized coating, so it's important to have tests run on water flowing from such pipes.

Red and yellow brass piping has threaded fittings and is found mostly in older homes. Red brass is 85 percent copper and 15 percent zinc and can last 75 years. Yellow brass contains less copper and has an average life expectancy of 40 years.

Plastic fittings are solvent-welded, compression-fitted, or threaded. Plastic piping can last a very long time since it does not rust or build up deposits. Some community building codes do not allow plastic piping because it can melt during a fire and give off toxic fumes. Common types of interior plastic piping include polyvinyl chloride (PVC), which is a white rigid pipe for cold-water, waste, and vent piping; chlorinated polyvinyl chloride (CPVC), which is a cream- or gray-colored rigid pipe suitable for hot and cold water; and polybutylene (PB), which is a gray flexible pipe for hot and cold water.

Shut-Off Valves

Some fixtures and appliances have their own shut-off valves so that work can be done on individual parts of the plumbing system without closing the main shut-off valve and disrupting water flow to the rest of the house (see figure 8.3).

Gate valves offer very little resistance to water flow and are used at the water heater or wherever there is only an occasional need to fully shut off water flow. They should be left in a fully open or fully closed position because water flowing against a partly open gate valve can damage it and cause leakage. Globe valves are installed wherever there is a need to control water flow, because they can remain partly open without damage. Stop-and-waste valves have removable side caps to allow water to drain from the pipes beyond the valves, a useful feature on exterior faucets to prevent freezing. Check valves have an internal hinged leaf that allows water to flow in only one direction; they are found anywhere there is a need to prevent backflow. Exterior water faucets are either globe valves or the frostproof type used in cold climates. Frostproof faucets shut off water flow inside the house and allow remaining water to drain out of the valve by gravity. Garden

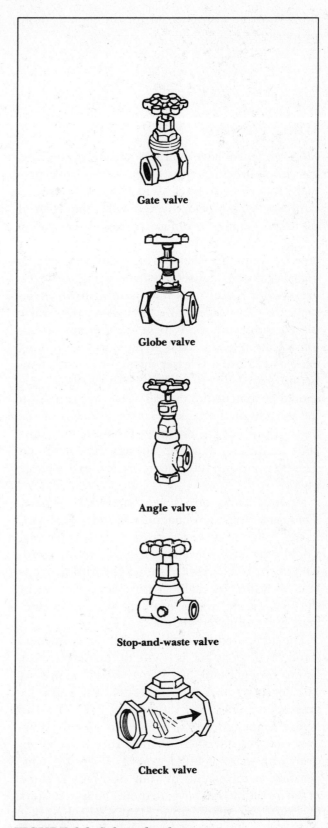

FIGURE 8.3 Selected valves

hoses must be disconnected for the pipe to drain properly.

Water Heaters

Most residences have their water heated by electric, gas-, or oil-fired heaters (see figure 8.4). Tanks normally range in size from 30 to 82 gallons. Modern tanks are "glass" lined, covered with a thin layer of porcelain enamel to reduce corrosion. Insulation is placed between the tank and the metal outer jacket to minimize heat loss and condensation. To guard against excessive pressures or temperatures, every water heater must have a pressure-and-temperature (P/T) relief valve. This is a safety valve placed within the top 6 inches of the tank. It automatically releases water if pressure in the tank exceeds 125 psi; it releases steam if the water temperature exceeds 210 degrees F. An extension pipe should be attached to the P/T valve and run down the outside of the tank to within 8 inches of the floor to prevent the discharge from burning anybody or causing damage. No impediment should prevent rapid and full drainage from this discharge pipe.

Modern tanks also have "sacrificial" anodes. These are replaceable magnesium rods suspended in the water to attract corrosive electrolytes that would otherwise consume the tank walls; electrolytes in the water react more readily with the rods than with the tank walls. A valve at the bottom of the tank allows periodic draining of water to eliminate any sediment buildup.

The temperature setting on all water heaters should be kept as low as is safe to conserve energy and to prolong tank life. Water should be at least 110 degrees F to kill microbes that can cause illness and no more than 120 degrees F, which is the hottest temperature most people can tolerate. However many dishwashers clean dishes most effectively with water at 140 degrees F. Check the temperature requirements of your dishwasher; some of the newer models have their own built-in heaters to boost water temperature. Many people find that their dishwashers clean adequately at lower temperatures.

Water Softeners

In some geographic areas water contains excessive amounts of calcium and magnesium, and is known as "hard" water. Hard water can leave a ring on bathroom fixtures and build up mineral deposits in water heaters and pipes. Water softeners can remove these minerals and replace them with sodium, which is less harmful to your plumbing system—but which, in your drinking water, may not be healthful for you. If you are concerned about excessive sodium in your diet, the softener can be connected to the water heater only, so that drinking water is not treated, or a line designated for drinking water can be run directly to the kitchen sink, thereby bypassing the softener.

The softener has two tanks. Untreated water first enters a mineral tank filled with plastic beads where the calcium and magnesium are exchanged for sodium. The second tank contains a sodium solution, or brine, that flushes the calcium and magnesium out of the mineral tank. This solution is then sent down a drain. In some communities the backwash from water softeners is not allowed in private septic systems and must be carted away.

Other types of filters and conditioners are available for a variety of conditions caused by water impurities or excessive minerals. Cloudy water, foul-tasting water, sulfurous water, corrosive water, and water with excessive amounts of iron can all be filtered. Depending on the type of filter or conditioner, the attachment will be to the main supply line or the cold-water pipe under the kitchen sink.

Drain-Waste System

Used water and wastes are carried to public sewage lines or to on-site disposal systems known as septic systems or cesspools through the drain and waste pipes (see figure 8.5). Horizontal pipes should be sloped ¼ inch per foot since the waste flows by gravity only. Slopes of ⅛ or ½ inch per foot are also permitted in some jurisdictions, but a steeper slope may cause blockages since it would allow water to outrun solid waste.

One of the most frequent calls to plumbers is for

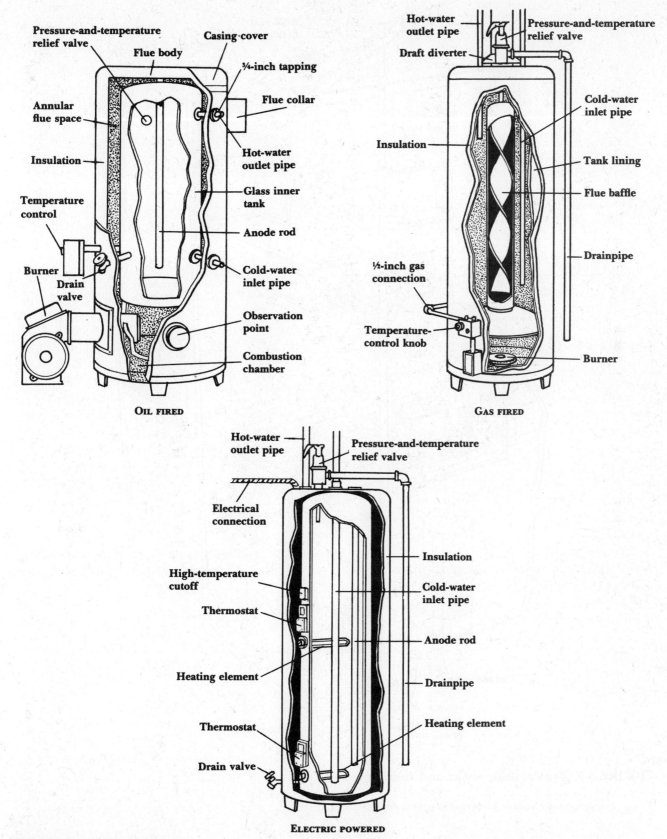

Pressure-and-temperature relief valve
Flue body
Casing cover
¾-inch tapping
Flue collar
Annular flue space
Hot-water outlet pipe
Insulation
Glass inner tank
Temperature control
Anode rod
Burner
Cold-water inlet pipe
Drain valve
Observation point
Combustion chamber

OIL FIRED

Hot-water outlet pipe
Pressure-and-temperature relief valve
Draft diverter
Cold-water inlet pipe
Insulation
Tank lining
Flue baffle
Drainpipe
½-inch gas connection
Temperature-control knob
Burner

GAS FIRED

Hot-water outlet pipe
Pressure-and-temperature relief valve
Electrical connection
Insulation
High-temperature cutoff
Cold-water inlet pipe
Thermostat
Anode rod
Heating element
Drainpipe
Thermostat
Heating element
Drain valve

ELECTRIC POWERED

FIGURE 8.4 Water heaters

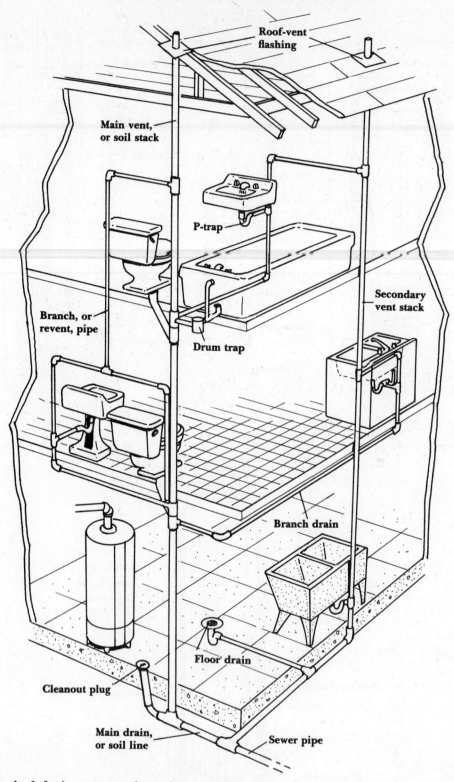

FIGURE 8.5 Typical drain-waste and venting systems

slow-draining fixtures and appliances. Slow-draining wastes are not just annoying but also potentially unhealthy. Most home inspectors consider a drain to be functional when it empties in a reasonable amount of time and does not overflow when one of its faucets is left on.

Drain, Waste, and Vent Piping

Drain, waste, and vent (DWV) systems can use any one or a combination of different pipe materials. Mixed systems in drain-waste piping will not cause the corrosive action that takes place in mixed water supply systems. Drain-waste pipes range in size from 1¼ to 4 inches in diameter, and are available in the following forms:

- Plastic piping comes in ABS (black) or PVC (white) plastic which can be solvent-welded, threaded, or secured with no-hub band clamps. Both ABS and PVC pipes can last a long time. Drain-waste plastic piping has to carry the National Sanitation Foundation (NSF) stamp to be suitable for these systems. ABS and PVC should not be solvent-welded together.
- Cast iron pipes are black or rust-colored and joined by oakum (hemp) and molten lead, plastic compression gaskets, or stainless steel no-hub fittings with neoprene sleeves. Cast iron pipes can slowly rust from the inside out.
- Galvanized iron pipes are gray with threaded fittings. They are similar to water supply pipes but larger in diameter. They can also rust from the inside out.
- Copper pipes have a yellow or red identification stripe and are usually used for aboveground drain-waste systems. The fittings are soldered or threaded.

Traps

The decomposing waste material in the sewage system emits objectionable and unhealthy odors known as sewer gases. To prevent sewer gases from flowing back into the house, each fixture drain has a U-shaped pipe called a trap (see figure 8.6). These are sometimes called P- or S-traps depending on their design. Bathtubs and showers in older houses may have drum traps located under the floor. A trap should always be filled with water to create a seal against sewer gases. Water draining out of the fixture will automatically fill the trap. Lack of proper venting can create a siphoning action that draws the water seal out of the trap, allowing sewer gases to enter the house. (S-traps are now illegal in most locales since they cannot be adequately vented.) Some older homes may have mechanical traps in which a gravity-operated valve closes to block sewer gases. Toilets do not need separate traps because traps are built into their bowls. Some homes may have a main house trap located near the foundation wall or under the front lawn to completely seal the entire system from the sewer.

Stacks

The main vertical drain line is called the soil stack. It is a 3-or 4-inch diameter pipe that accepts wastes directly from the toilet and from all other fixtures through branch drain lines. The soil stack also serves as a vent, as discussed later.

Cleanouts are plugged openings found along drain lines and in some traps to facilitate removal of blockages with a plumber's snake or auger. A cleanout may also surface in the grounds outside the house to provide access for cleaning out blockage farther down the sewer line.

When fixtures are located below the lowest drain point, such as in some basement bathrooms, wastes are sometimes gathered in a container and pumped up to the house sewer by an extractor or ejector pump.

Vent System

Venting is necessary to maintain equal atmospheric pressure within the drain-waste pipe system and to safely dispose of sewer gases outside the house (see figure 8.5). Without air in the drain pipes, water seals in the traps would be siphoned off and sewer

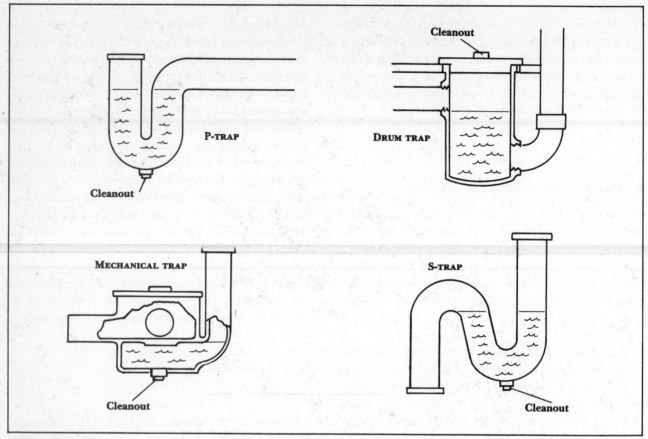

FIGURE 8.6 Traps

gases would enter the home through the drains. *All plumbing fixtures must be vented.* In some older homes it is not uncommon to find inadequate venting caused by obsolete S-traps, or a single main trap installed in the sewer line, where it is very susceptible to blockages.

The vent pipes are connected to the drain-waste system at each fixture's drain line downstream from the trap, which is called back venting. The main soil stack extends out the roof and vents toilets. Other fixtures may have their own vent pipes protruding through the roof or may be vented into the main soil stack, provided they are vented above the highest fixture served by that stack, which is called branch venting or reventing. Where it is not possible to run a vent pipe out the roof, some communities allow mechanical vents. Mechanical vents act like flap valves, opening to allow water to drain out and snapping shut to prevent sewer gases from coming up the drain.

Cross Connections

A cross connection in the plumbing system is any point where contaminated water or wastes might mix with potable water. A sudden drop in water pressure—resulting from a water-main break, for example—could draw contaminated water or wastes into the freshwater supply system if there is a cross connection. This presents a serious health hazard. Some examples of cross connections are points where a sink or bathtub spout is below the flood rim of those fixtures; or a toilet ballcock valve is under water; or nonpotable irrigation water pipes are connected to the water supply system; or where a garden hose is left in a hot tub, swimming pool, or gutter (see figure 8.7). A swing check valve, or vacuum breaker, can be installed on exterior water faucets to prevent the last occurrence. The valve closes when water starts to flow in the reverse direction.

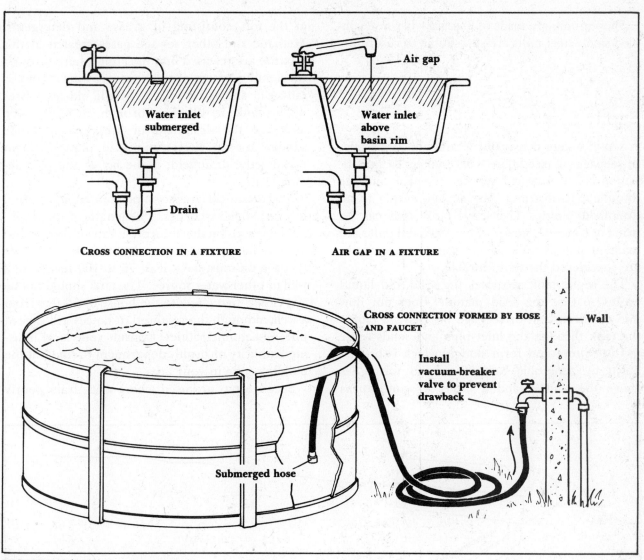

FIGURE 8.7 Cross connections

Plumbing Fixtures

Toilets are usually made of vitreous china. Their operation appears to be very complicated to most people, but in reality it is quite simple. When the tank handle is pushed or lifted, a connecting rod raises a rubber stopper from a valve at the bottom of the tank. Water from the tank rushes into the bowl as the tank's float ball drops with the water level. As water fills the bowl, gravity and a siphoning action draw the contents of the bowl through the trap and into the drainage system. After the tank water is released, the rubber stopper drops down to seal the valve at the bottom of the tank. Water from the supply line flows through a ballcock valve to refill the bowl and then the tank. When the water in the tank reaches the proper level, the float ball rises on an arm that shuts off the ballcock valve.

Bathtubs are made of fiberglass, reinforced plastic, enameled steel, or enameled cast iron. The fiberglass units are available in one-piece shower/tub units and eliminate the need for wall protection. Plastic tubs are easy to clean, but they scratch easily. Plastic tubs and shower stalls tend to give under the weight of a person, and this flexing action can cause the caulking around drains to loosen or the tub to crack. Steel and cast iron are long lasting but can develop surface chips and may even rust under extreme conditions.

Shower units are made of fiberglass, tile, or enameled steel. Steel units are susceptible to rusting.

Septic Systems

A septic system consists of a tank and drainfield, or seepage pit (see figure 8.8). Sometimes a distribution box is installed between the tank and the drainfield to distribute the sewage evenly to all drainfield piping. The septic tank itself can be made of concrete, steel, or fiberglass, and tanks are made in 500- to 1,500-gallon sizes. Concrete tanks are considered the most durable.

The septic tank separates the solid and liquid wastes so that the solid material does not flow into the drainfield or seepage pit. Sewage enters the tank through the inlet pipe and solids settle to the bottom and form sludge, which is broken down by anaerobic bacteria. Liquid waste lies above the sludge, and a layer of scum forms at the top, consisting of grease and detergents. Methane and other sewage gases created in this mixture are released into the atmosphere through the venting system of the house. A working septic tank will always be full. As the liquid level rises in the tank, it will flow through an outlet pipe and into the drainfield or seepage pit. Some systems use an ejector pump to pump effluent up into the drainfield, if the lay of the plot demands it.

The drainfield consists of perforated pipe buried in gravel-filled trenches. The length of the drainfield depends on the absorption rate of the soil and local building codes. Usually, the drainfield or seepage pit must be at least 75 to 100 feet from a well or other water source. The tank should not be any closer than 5 feet to the house or 50 feet from a well, although the required distances will vary in different municipalities. Consult your local housing authority or health department to find out the building code in your area.

Seepage pits are used where soils drain poorly

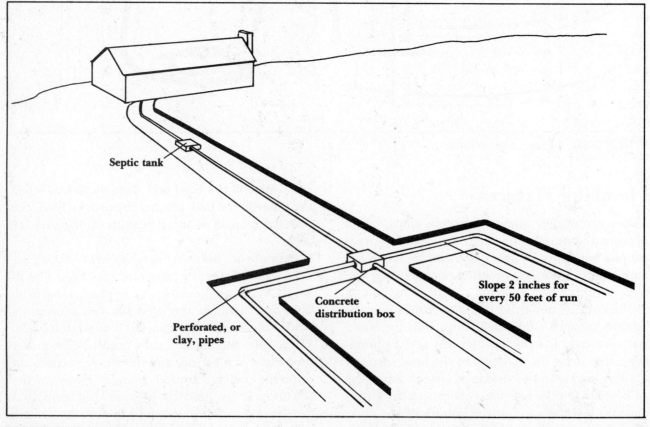

FIGURE 8.8 Septic system

or when a building site does not have enough area for a drainfield. The septic tank's output pipe runs to the seepage pit. The pit is lined with a perforated masonry liner or stones that disperse the effluent to be absorbed by the soil.

In regions with heavy, clay soils, some homes have a mechanical or oxidizing septic system. Motor-driven impellers force air down into the contents of the septic tank, and aerobic bacteria feed on the sludge. The effluent is pure and can run directly into open ditches, streams, and ponds.

If properly installed and maintained, a septic system should work properly for 20 years or more. If the system was inspected during installation, your local building or sanitation department may have the inspection records and the exact location of the system on your property.

Inspecting Plumbing

Many elements of the plumbing system can be checked by most homeowners. If you do not feel comfortable or knowledgeable enough to inspect a particular item, consult with an inspector, engineer, or licensed plumber. Defects or shortcomings that you discover should be discussed with those professionals.

Warning: Do not confuse plumbing pipes with gas or warm water (hydronic) heating systems. Familiarize yourself with those systems before doing any work on plumbing systems.

You will need a flashlight, magnet, carpenter's level (no longer than 12 inches) or bullet level, towel, notepad, and pen. To avoid confusion, each section of the plumbing system will be listed below under a separate heading. These systems can be inspected separately or together. Consult Table 8.1 as an aid to your inspection.

Wells

If you receive your drinking water from a well, the following checks should be made, but bear in mind that most problems with wells will need to be corrected by a professional.

First, locate the well head. If visible, it should be tightly sealed or capped off to prevent contamination. If you live in a cold climate and have an above-ground pump, the pump shed should be insulated and heated to prevent the pump and water lines from freezing.

The well pump has a pressure gauge, which must function properly. If the pump comes on for just a small demand of water, such as filling a pitcher, the pressure tank may be waterlogged. If the pressure tank is "sweating" (covered with condensation), it may need to be insulated. It is a good idea to have a licensed electrician check the pump wiring for safety.

The pumping system must be capable of providing enough water pressure and water volume for your needs. This can best be checked by a plumber or a licensed well or pump contractor.

Sand or dirt in your toilet tank may indicate that the pump screen is damaged and needs replacement. Their presence can also be a sign that the well may not be deep enough or in a good location. Barring drilling another well, which may be prohibitively expensive, you may need to install a special water filter to remove the grit from the water supply.

Water Supply Pipes

Enter the crawl space or basement to locate the main water shut-off valve. This valve is sometimes located outside the house. Do *not* turn the valve to make sure it works, since the valve stem may start leaking if the valve has not been operated for a long time. Simply note the main shut-off location and have a plumber test the valve the next time you call one in for any reason. If leakage does develop when your plumber checks it, it is usually because the valve stem packing needs to be replaced. Repairs can be carried out after the water is shut off at the street or in the pump house. An inoperable valve should be repaired or replaced since it is of no value.

Try to determine what type of pipe was installed between the street and the house. A short section of this pipe is usually visible between the main valve

TABLE 8.1 The Plumbing System

WATER SUPPLY SYSTEM

Problem	Possible Causes	Remedies
No water flow	Water supply system is off	Check main valve or power to well
	Leaking or frozen pipe	Repair or thaw
	Defective water softener	Consult serviceman
	Clogged water filter	Clean filter
Decreased flow	Above causes	Same as above
	Sink faucet aerator is clogged	Clean aerator screen
	Corrosion or mineral deposits in piping	Replace those pipe sections as needed
Water hammer	No air chamber	Consult plumber
	Waterclogged chambers	Drain system as described
	Pipes not secured	Add hangars/straps
Frostproof faucet is frozen	Water supply pipe is not sloped down to faucet	Thaw and reposition pipe
	Garden hose left attached	Remove hose during winter
Stains or deposits on fixtures	Minerals in water	Filter or treat water
	Rusting or corroding pipes	Consult plumber

DRAIN-WASTE SYSTEM

Problem	Possible Causes	Remedies
Slow-draining fixtures	Blockage or deposits in trap or drain pipes	Use plunger, plumber's snake, or replace pipes
	Lack of vent	Consult plumber
	Inadequate pipe slope	Consult plumber
	Problems with septic system	Consult septic contractor

VENT SYSTEM

Problem	Possible Causes	Remedies
Smell of sewer gas	Loss of water seal on trap	Check venting
	Drain(s) has an S-trap	Consult plumber
	Broken vent pipe or vent pipe terminates inside house	Consult plumber
	Blockage in vent pipe	Flush with hose
Gurgling in drains	Incorrect size of drain pipe	Consult plumber
	Improper venting	Consult plumber
Blockage in vent pipe	Debris	Flush with hose
	Frozen vapors in pipe located outside	Protect from freezing

and the foundation wall. If yours is an older home and a lead pipe was used, the water should be tested by a certified laboratory, as noted earlier.

Note the type of water supply piping used inside the house. Use your magnet to differentiate galvanized iron pipe from copper or brass. If both copper *and* galvanized iron were used, inspect the points of contact between the dissimilar materials to see if dielectric or brass fittings were used. If not, plan to discuss corrections with a plumber.

If PVC plastic piping has been used in conjunction with metal piping, special transition unions should have been used since the two materials expand and contract at different rates. Clamps should be secure where they have been used on plastic fittings. You can tighten loose clamps yourself with a screwdriver or wrench. Check the stamped ratings on all plastic pipes to make sure they are rated to withstand house water pressures of 20 to 80 psi and that plastic pipes carrying hot water are rated for that use.

Water pipes must also be adequately supported by the floor joists or wall studs. Copper and plastic piping should be supported every 4 feet; galvanized piping every 5 feet. Plan to install additional support where needed. Check the existing pipe straps and hangers to make sure they are compatible with the piping. In particular, copper pipe should have rubber or nylon straps, never galvanized metal. Copper should not be in contact with steel beams, heating ducts, nails, or other dissimilar metals. If you notice corrosion or mineral deposits on the outside of any metal pipe or joint, there is a leak in the making. Consult with a plumber to find out whether replacement is necessary at this time. Copper tubing should not feel soft when squeezed. If it does, the tubing may be corroding from the inside out and should be replaced.

Obviously, wherever you look, check for leaks. Inspect all pipes and fittings closely. But do not confuse "sweating" pipes with leaking pipes. Water droplets will sometimes form on metal pipes in humid locations such as basements and crawl spaces. Wipe off wet pipes with a towel to see if a leak is really occurring. A leak will start dripping again almost immediately; condensation takes time to form.

The water meter can be of value in proving that a hidden or slow leak exists. After your inspection or at a convenient time, turn off all faucets and appliances. Then use a felt-tipped pen to mark the location of the needles on all scales of the water meter, and do not operate any fixture or appliance for a few hours. If any of the needles move, there is a leak in the system and you will need to investigate further to locate it (see chapter 6).

While looking at the system, make a note of any pipes that have been patched. Patched pipes should be checked periodically for leaks, or replaced with new pipe, since patches are meant to be temporary.

Using your level, see if the pipes are sloped downward toward the main shut-off valve. Be aware that if supply pipes are not properly sloped, it will be very difficult to completely drain the pipes, if that ever becomes necessary. Although repair work at that time will be more expensive, it's not worth replacing improperly sloped supply pipes.

If your basement or crawl space is not heated and you live in a cold climate, the pipes should be insulated or wrapped with electrical heating cable to prevent freezing. This is especially important where the pipes are installed close to basement windows, foundation vents, or uninsulated walls.

The Water Heater

Inspection of the water heater should start at the hot and cold water lines attached to the tank. Carefully touch each pipe to distinguish the hot water and cold water lines. The proper tank connections for each line are usually stamped on the water heater's outer metal jacket.

Look at the top of the tank to see whether metal piping (as opposed to plastic) has been used for at least the first 12 inches above the water heater, and inspect for corrosion or leakage at the pipe joints. Repairs should be carried out before severe leaks occur. A shut-off valve on the cold water line to the tank will facilitate repairs without forcing you to shut off water to the entire house. It might be wise to have such a valve installed if it doesn't exist.

As mentioned earlier, a water heater should have both a pressure *and* a temperature relief valve with ratings that match the tank specifications. Check both the P/T valve and the water heater specification plates. The P/T valve should be installed within the top 6 inches of the tank, or in the hot water pipe no more than 6 inches above the tank. The relief valve should also have a drain tube to safely divert overflow to the floor or a drain. The discharge tube should have the same inside diameter as the relief valve outlet; a tube with a smaller diameter will restrict flow. There must not be any valve or cap on the discharge tube or any other restriction that will prevent rapid drainage. Check periodically to see whether any water has been discharging through the relief valve. This would indicate a problem with the water heater or the relief valve that should be investigated immediately by a plumber.

Carefully inspect the water heater's outer metal jacket for rust or signs of leakage. A leaking water heater almost always has to be replaced, since there is no way to make a repair. Some heaters will form condensation, which could be mistaken for leakage. Use your towel to wipe the moist areas to determine whether leaks are actually occurring.

If you have a gas- or oil-fired water heater, and if you hear popping or crackling noises, sediment has built up and should be drained off through the valve at the bottom of the tank into a bucket. The combustion area of these heaters should also be clean. Scales or corrosion particles at the bottom of the tank or in the combustion area may indicate that cleaning is needed or that the tank is rusting.

Upstairs Fixtures and Plumbing

It's a good idea to combine the following checks with the inspection of the upstairs drain and waste system discussed later in this chapter.

Check the operation of all faucets and shut-off valves, and examine exposed pipes for leaks. Turn on all the faucets in a room, and let them run about half a minute. Water flow should be strong when more than one faucet or fixture operates at the same time. Low pressure may indicate that corrosion or mineral deposits are building up inside the pipes. A plumber may be able to quickly determine how extensive the clogging is and which pipes are suspect.

As you turn off the faucets, listen for water hammering. Try to ascertain whether air chamber de-

vices were installed, although this is difficult since they are normally hidden from view inside the walls. If you do find air chambers and water hammering still occurs, the chambers are probably waterlogged. Air can be restored to the chambers by following the procedure for draining the water supply system as described later in this chapter.

Next, test all sink and toilet shut-off valves to make certain they work well. Open the valves fully, then close them a quarter turn to prolong their useful life.

Look at each faucet spout or tub spigot to see if they are below the flood rim of the basin. In that case, a cross connection could result, so a different type of faucet or spigot must be installed.

All plumbing fixtures—tubs, shower stalls, sinks, basins, and toilets—should be free of cracks, rust, or other forms of surface damage. There are specialists who can resurface or patch fixtures, unless complete replacement is warranted. Stains may indicate that water treatment is necessary, although some toilet stains occur because the toilet is rarely used (try household cleaners before taking more drastic action). Fixtures must be firmly attached to the wall or floor, especially wall-hung sinks and toilets. Caulk and putty seals should be in good condition (see chapter 6). An inexpensive tube of caulk, properly applied, can prevent expensive repairs to surrounding surfaces.

Carefully lift up the tank lid of your toilet, and check to see that the ballcock valve is not totally immersed in water. A ballcock valve that is under water makes a cross connection, which must be corrected by installing a valve with a taller tube or by lowering the water level in the tank. If the toilet tank "sweats," consider installing an insulated foam liner inside the tank to prevent cold water from coming into contact with the tank body. These liners are usually available from hardware or plumbing-supply stores. In extreme cases, a hot water pipe will have to be run to the toilet and a tempering valve installed to provide lukewarm water to the tank. Of course, every toilet should flush completely and shut off properly.

Outside Faucets

See whether the exterior water faucets are of the frostproof type. If not, and if you live in a cold climate, there should be an interior stop-and-waste valve to prevent freezing. If you do not have either of these frost protections, it would be wise to install one or the other. If you have frostproof faucets, the pipe serving the faucets should have a downward slope to allow proper drainage when the valve is shut off. Place your level on the pipe serving this faucet, or visually determine whether water drains out of the faucet as it is shut off. All outside faucets should be firmly attached to the exterior wall to prevent the piping and fittings inside the house from twisting. Where garden hoses are used to fill hot tubs or pools, or to clean gutters, their faucets should have swing check valves (vacuum breakers) to prevent siphoning and backflow if there is ever a sudden drop in water pressure. These valves are usually available from plumbing-supply stores.

Drains and Sewage

Begin your inspection of this system inside the basement or crawl space, and note what type of drain and waste pipes were installed. (Again, these procedures can be combined with the inspection of the water supply if you feel confident of your abilities.) All drain and waste pipes should have a downward slope of ¼ inch per foot. This can be easily determined with your level. Pipes should slope uniformly and not sag or exhibit low spots where the flow of waste would be slowed down or impeded. Pipes should also be securely fastened and supported: cast iron pipe should be supported every 5 feet, whereas plastic piping should be supported every 4 feet because it is less rigid. Plastic pipes should be specifically designed for use on drain-waste systems. Look for the "NSF" markings on the pipe required by the National Sanitation Foundation. Carefully check all pipes for leaks, cracks, or open areas. Look under bathrooms, the laundry room, and the kitchen for leaks after an assistant operates the fixtures in those rooms. All leaks should be repaired as soon as possible.

If drain-line cleanouts have not been provided under the house, it will be difficult to remove any blockage that develops in the sewer line. Cleanouts should be securely capped off with removable plugs. Plugs that are cracked or otherwise damaged should be replaced, since sewer gases can seep out of any openings.

If you live in a cold climate, look at the areas surrounding drain-line traps to see whether nearby windows, foundation vents, or uninsulated walls create cold spots where standing water in the trap might freeze. Those areas can be blocked off or insulated to prevent the entry of cold air.

If your basement has a sump pump, make sure it is connected to a storm drain, not to a septic-tank or sewage system. Those systems are not capable of handling large amounts of water at one time. A plumber is best suited to make any necessary corrections.

Upstairs Drains

Walk through the house and run water through all the sinks to check for leaks underneath. It's convenient to check drains while you test water flow, as discussed earlier; a flashlight is helpful. While looking in the cabinet under the kitchen sink, see if the dishwasher has an air gap device, which is required in some communities. If there is no air gap device, the dishwasher drain tube must be securely fastened and should have a looped section of pipe that rises higher than the top of the dishwasher. This prevents a cross connection and waste water from siphoning back into the machine. In the laundry room, check the washing machine's drain tube. It too must at some point rise above the highest water level in the machine to prevent reverse siphoning.

Listen for gurgling sounds when water drains through the sinks. This may indicate that the sink is not properly vented. If you find slow-draining fixtures, their drain lines may need cleaning, something most homeowners can do. Avoid chemical drain cleaners; most are extremely caustic and can cause burns and severe eye damage—even blindness. Mechanical devices such as the traditional plumber's "helper" (called a plumber's plunger, face cut, or force pump) or drain auger (called a plumber's snake) can clear clogged drains effectively and safely; pour boiling water down the drains every week or so to help keep them clean.

Look carefully at the ceilings under all plumbing fixtures for leaks. Look at all the drain traps; in particular, look for fixtures that do not have traps. (Be aware that some washing machine drain-line traps are located inside the wall.) Have S-traps replaced if you find them.

The Vent System

The inspection of the vent system begins outside the house. There should be vent pipes protruding through the roof, or placed alongside the walls in older homes. If you do not see any vent pipes, or suspect that a fixture is not vented, discuss it with a plumber. If vents terminate in front of windows, they should be extended or rerouted so that vapors do not enter the house. Vent pipes should protrude above the roof by at least 6 inches, higher in snowy climates.

If you live in a cold climate, vents placed against an outside wall, if less than 3 inches in diameter, are susceptible to blockage, since vapors inside the pipes can freeze and block the air flow. These vent pipes should be insulated and surrounded by a wood-framed enclosure where possible.

Many local building authorities require that a main-house trap have a vent with a screened air inlet. The inlet is usually visible in the foundation wall above the trap, or may have a gooseneck fitting. If your home has a main-house trap but you cannot find a vent for it, ask a plumber to install one; otherwise the trap's water seal may be lost.

Complete the inspection of the vent system indoors. Look for vent pipes that terminate inside the house, basement, crawl space, or attic (see chapter 2). Since sewer vapors can be very unhealthy to inhale, all vent pipes must terminate outside the house. Any necessary corrections should be made as soon as possible.

The Septic System

Record the exact location of your home's sewer line, septic tank, distribution box (if installed), and the drainfield or seepage pit. If you cannot physically locate the system, check with the local building department or health department, which may have this information on record.

With a long tape measure, confirm that the tank is at least 50 feet from a well and at least 5 feet from any building. The drainfield or seepage pit should be at least 75 to 100 feet from a well. As mentioned, all these distances may vary with your local code; check with your local building authority before taking measurements. If buildings or roads have been built over the tank or drainfield, discuss the possible problems with the health department. Tree roots sometimes penetrate the sewer line or drainfield. Sewer lines may need periodic routing; a tree surgeon may have to remove roots or even entire trees.

It would be useful to know when the septic tank or seepage pit was last pumped out, as well as its present condition. A septic-tank pumping service can determine the condition of the tank after it has been pumped out. Save the evaluation for the next time the tank is pumped. You should check for seepage or foul odors over the tank or drainfield. Before the tank is pumped, walk over the system and field soon after at least several hundred gallons of water have been run into the tank (each person in the family uses about 100 gallons per day). Be alert for odors. Odors around a septic tank may point to a leaky tank. A drainfield that emits odors and has soggy soil may have reached the end of its useful life. Over time, a drainfield becomes saturated with waste and effluent, and must be relocated—an expensive undertaking. Read Chapter 11, and consult at least three septic-system specialists before proceeding with such a project.

In general the discharge ends of gutter downspouts, like sump pumps and other house storm drains, should not be connected to septic systems or municipal sewage disposal systems, although this depends on local codes.

Keeping the Water Flowing

Most homeowners should not find it beyond their ability to perform some routine plumbing maintenance tasks and thereby avoid more costly repairs in the future.

In the basement and along the water supply system, operate individual shut-off valves (*not* the main shut-off) at least once a year to keep the valve packing flexible and to prevent the buildup of corrosion. Leave valves one quarter turn less than fully open to extend their life.

Drain a few gallons from the water heater every 6 months to prevent the accumulation of sediment. Your owner's manual should contain a procedure for draining the water heater. If not, consult a plumber. More frequently—every month—inspect the pressure-and-temperature relief valve for overflow, which indicates excessive pressure or temperature for safe operation. Once a year trip the valve's release lever, but be prepared to shut off the water supply to the tank if the valve doesn't close fully. In that case, it needs to be cleaned or replaced.

Older heaters need more frequent inspections, especially for leaks. Gas-fired water heaters should be serviced by a professional every other year, whereas oil-fired heaters should be serviced annually. In particular, the professional should check that flue gases are venting up the chimney properly.

If you've discovered that the air chambers of your plumbing contain water, the procedure for flushing them and restoring the air pockets begins in the basement. If you have an electric water heater, shut the power off. Shut off the main water supply valve. Be prepared to call in a plumber if the valve starts leaking. Open and drain all faucets and appliances, and flush all the toilets. Open the drain plug or plugs, which will be located near the main water shut-off valve or at some other low point in the system. (If the basement has no drain, you'll need to use buckets.) When the system is completely drained, it will fill with air through the open faucets. Now close the faucets and slowly open the main valve to refill the system. Switch power to the water heater back on. Check and make certain all faucets are closed and no leaks are visible anywhere.

Throughout the house generally, every month, clean pop-up drains and strainers, faucet and sink sprayer aerators and diverters, and try to keep fat, grease, and coffee grounds out of drains and dishwashers. The same goes for paints and chemicals—never pour them down drains. They can damage pipes and septic systems. As mentioned, a pot of boiling water poured down each drain every month helps keep them clear. Appliance filters should be cleaned and/or replaced according to manufacturer's recommendations. Every month flush your garbage disposal with one pot of hot water and one half cup of baking soda. During regular use, always flush the disposal with cold water and grind small amounts of garbage at a time.

Every few months clean the dishwasher's air gap device and food strainer, and clean food particles from the holes in the spray arm. Clean the washing machine's hose screens as frequently. Follow manufacturer's recommended procedures for maintaining water softeners.

Before each winter in cold regions, drain all outside faucets that are not the frostproof type after closing off the interior shut-off valve, if there is one. Remove garden hoses and store them indoors. Check all frostproof valves to ensure that they shut off completely.

You may consider installing water-saving devices on all faucets to limit the amount of water that enters the septic system.

Professional Help

Plumbers are expensive. They have to go through extensive schooling and testing before they can get a license. A plumber's license and insurance fees are costly, and plumbers must also maintain large inventories. Moreover, they're in great demand. But most homeowners who have attempted major plumbing repairs do not complain much about plumber's fees. They usually vow that a plumber will be called in next time. Doing it yourself is hard, frustrating work—sometimes in damp, dark spaces—and may involve countless trips to the hardware store to get that "one" other fitting that is needed to complete the job.

On the other hand, many plumbers would rather see homeowners make minor repairs, such as changing washers, repairing toilets, and unclog-ging drains. They prefer to be called on for the bigger jobs and more complex tasks. Major repairs require skill, knowledge, tools, and time, and must satisfy local codes.

Some routine maintenance is best performed by a plumber. Don't check mechanical traps yourself, since they are prone to failure and difficult to in-spect. Ejector pumps should be serviced every year by a professional, and checked every 6 months for proper operation. Have a licensed plumber look at mechanical vents about once a year.

Well water should be fully tested by a qualified laboratory at least once a year. The pump, pressure switch, storage tank, and related equipment should also be professionally serviced periodically. Hire a professional pumping service to inspect, and if nec-essary, pump out the septic tank or seepage pit every two to four years, depending on the number of house occupants.

Preventive maintenance is always less expen-sive than repair or replacement of something that has broken down. So resist the temptation to do without the above maintenance work or to cut financial corners by trying to do the difficult tasks yourself.

9

HEATING

Heating systems are classified according to the fuel they burn and the method used to distribute heat. For example, a gas-fired, forced-air system burns gas to produce heat and distributes the heat throughout the house by forcing hot air through ducts. An oil-fired, steam system, on the other hand, burns oil to produce heat and distributes it in the form of steam moving through the radiators. A hot-water system, which may be fired by oil or gas, distributes heat by circulating hot water. Hot-water and forced-air heating systems can also be electrically heated by large resistance coils, but this is uncommon. Electric baseboard heating is usually controlled locally and is not considered to be a central system.

In the case of a steam or hot-water heating system, fuel is burned in the boiler. The life expectancy of a cast-iron boiler is from 35 to 50 years; the newer steel boilers last from 15 to 25 years. In hot air systems, the heating unit is called a furnace, which has an average life expectancy of 15 to 25 years.

Central Heating

Heating systems differ in how they work, but since the principle of central heating is basic to all of them—heat originates at one source and is distributed throughout the house—different types of systems have a few common features.

The Burner

All heating systems that use gas or oil as a fuel burn this fuel in a combustion chamber, or fire box. Oil fuel is injected into the combustion chamber by an oil or fuel gun powered by an electric motor. An oil gun mixes droplets of oil with air and then shoots this mixture into the combustion chamber under pressure, very much like a perfume atomizer or carburetor. Oil systems use an electrode, which works like a spark plug, to ignite the fuel. Gas enters the combustion chamber either under its own line pressure, just as gas enters the kitchen stove, or under boosted pressure. Gas systems use an electrode or pilot light to ignite the gas when the furnace or boiler turns on. Pilot lights are protected

---

by a draft diverter, which is a system of baffles that prevents the blower from extinguishing the pilot light.

Safety Devices

In an oil-burning system, if the thermostat calls for the heating system to come on, and fuel enters the system but does not ignite, highly flammable and explosive fuel spews into the combustion chamber and creates a dangerous situation. To prevent this from continuing, one or more of the following cut-off devices are used in oil burning boilers and furnaces. A flame tester operates like an electric "eye" and automatically shuts down the system if it senses no flame (light) in the combustion chamber after oil is pumped in. A stack relay senses temperature in the flue and shuts off the system if temperature remains low after the boiler or furnace kicks on and fails to ignite. A system that has been shut off by the flame tester or stack relay will not operate again until a reset button is pressed.

Pressing the reset button is one of the few troubleshooting procedures the homeowner can safely perform in trying to get a nonfunctioning oil system to work. However, if a safety device shuts down the system twice, the system must be serviced by a professional. In short: Never press the reset button more than once in an attempt to get a system to work.

All gas-fired systems have a safety device called a thermocouple. It shuts the gas off if the pilot light goes out or the thermocouple is defective.

The Thermostat

Familiar to all homeowners, this temperature-sensitive device contains metal elements that close an electrical circuit at a set minimum temperature and turn on the heating system. When a set maximum temperature is reached, the circuit opens and the system shuts down. Clock thermostats have a small clock that can be adjusted so the system maintains a lower temperature during the night, thus conserving energy. Multiple-setback thermostats permit even more complex and frequent temperature-setting changes, and may be desirable if no one is home during the day.

An Essential Safety Inspection

Every month during the heating season, examine an oil-burning system for signs of "puff backs." These are black soot stains around the doors of the boiler or furnace, or at the seams of the flue pipe where it enters the boiler or furnace. If such signs appear, it is imperative that a professional repair person correct the problem; puff backs indicate a fire hazard exists, poisonous gases are escaping into the house, or both.

Examine the flue pipe of an oil- or gas-burning system for soot, holes, or corrosion. Call a professional to correct these conditions.

Professional and Do-It-Yourself Maintenance

The professional heating contractor is the best person to take care of regular servicing, particularly those items in each system recommended for annual or semi-annual performance checks. Not only will the professional perform the specific tasks you request; he or she should adjust the entire system for optimal operation.

When you do those homeowner's tasks suggested for each system, always shut off electric power to the heating system so that the system doesn't operate unexpectedly. When you have completed your tasks, remember to turn the system back on.

Use a vacuum to clean every thermostat every 3 months, but be careful. The mechanism is fragile and should remain level. Vacuum radiators, baseboard units, and heat registers about every month so that they remain free of dust and radiate heat efficiently.

On oil systems, examine the fuel gun and lubricate it three times a year if there are exposed lubrication points.

Chimneys used in oil-fired systems should be cleaned by a professional chimney sweep every other year to prevent the accumulation of incompletely burned materials. These can cause chimney fires. Furthermore, it is possible for debris to build up at the base of the chimney, and this could block the passage of flue gases on their way up. Buildup in gas-fired systems is less of a problem and need only be evaluated periodically by a chimney sweep.

Hot-Air Systems

A forced-air furnace in a typical small residence burns either gas or Number 2 fuel oil. This produces hot gases that pass through a heat exchanger (see figure 9.1). The heat exchanger transfers heat to clean air while keeping that air separated from the hot flue gases, which may contain carbon monoxide and can be lethal if allowed to accumulate in the home. The flue gases, after giving up much of their heat, are directed up the flue and out the chimney. The warmed air is blown through the plenum and the house ductwork by a blower, or basket fan.

After reaching the rooms through outlet vents, called supply registers, the air cools and is drawn back to the furnace through return registers. At the furnace, the air is again heated and distributed throughout the house. Somewhere in the system, usually at the point where returning air enters the furnace, a filter or two is positioned to clean the air.

Forced-air heating systems are also equipped with automatic blower-control switches. It is usually undesirable for the blower to come on immediately after the house thermostat calls for heat, because this would only circulate cool air around the house. Instead, a setting on the blower-control switch keeps the blower off until the air near the heat exchanger reaches a preset temperature. A different setting on the blower control keeps the blower on for a while after the furnace turns off. The furnace is still very hot, and it would warp and buckle if the blower did not continue to force air through it.

Limit switches are safety devices that shut down the furnace when the temperature inside the heat exchanger exceeds the maximum allowable, usually 205 degrees F.

Since the air coming from a forced-air system is inherently dry, many systems are equipped with humidifiers. Different types of humidifiers are available, the most effective being an electrically operated model that sells for about $300 to $500 installed. It puts controlled amounts of moisture into the air. The drip type and other similar humidifiers, although appreciably less expensive, don't permit as precise control, and may not provide an acceptable level of comfort. They may also cause premature corrosion of the heat exchanger by allowing too much water into the system.

Inspection

Inspect your forced-air heating system twice a year, at the beginning of and midway through the heating season.

A good sense of smell is an important tool in inspections of heating systems. If you ever detect the odor of oil or gas anywhere in the house, turn off the system and contact a heating contractor immediately. Fuel odors may be due to an ignition failure caused by a simultaneous malfunctioning of the pilot light or electric ignition and failure of the safety shutdown elements. Odors are more likely to be noticed in an oil-fired system than a gas-fired one, since natural gas is lighter than air and tends to vent up the flue. Fuel odors indicate a hazardous and potentially deadly condition. Don't delay having this situation investigated.

Likewise, the odor of flue gases should be looked into and corrected immediately. This odor can be caused by a blocked chimney or flue pipe, or a damaged heat exchanger. Dark stains appearing around the room registers are a more subtle symptom of these problems. Another sign is excessive condensation, especially noticeable around windows, because a major component of flue gas is water vapor. This could signal a leak in the heat exchanger or flue that requires immediate repair.

Begin your investigation by taking a close look at the furnace. Listen to it as well. If you hear unusual clunking or growling noises while the blower is on, the problem might be worn fan bearings or a loose or defective fan belt. These noises could indicate either the need for relatively simple

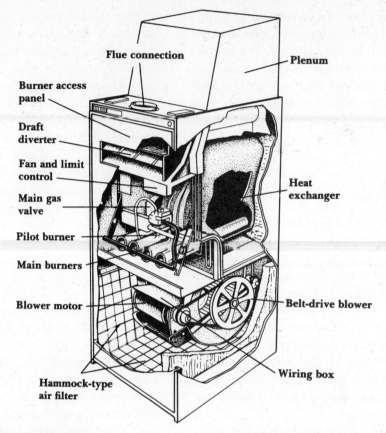

Flue connection — Plenum

Burner access panel

Draft diverter

Fan and limit control

Main gas valve

Pilot burner

Main burners

Heat exchanger

Blower motor — Belt-drive blower

Wiring box

Hammock-type air filter

FIGURE 9.1 Upflow hot-air furnace

repairs or, possibly, the imminent failure of the heating system. Call in a reliable heating contractor; a professional will know the difference. You may wish to hire an impartial consultant if you're uncertain about the necessity of expensive repairs.

Examine the humidifier carefully. Humidifiers are notorious for small leaks that cause large damage. A constant drip from a humidifier, even if slow, can cause major corrosion of and damage to the heat exchanger and ductwork of a forced-air heating system.

Check exposed ductwork for air leaks. Ductwork can be most easily inspected in the cellar and the attic. You can usually spot separations between sections of ductwork. Feel around suspect joints. Also feel around the heat registers throughout the house. Air escaping around the edge of a grille indicates that heated air is being forced into the walls—a waste of energy. In most cases bringing the two duct sections together and binding them with duct tape or pushing the grille firmly into place is all that is necessary to stop leaks.

You can test whether there is adequate air flow from the registers by holding a piece of paper in front of each vent. The force of the air should lift the paper. When repeating this procedure at a later date, you may notice an appreciably lower rate of air flow. Examine the filter to see if it is clogged with dirt and therefore in need of replacement. To ensure proper air flow, make sure that no furniture blocks the registers.

Maintenance of the Hot-Air System

Before any maintenance is done on your heating system, shut off electric power to the furnace so that it doesn't fire up unexpectedly, and motors don't suddenly begin moving. The maintenance tasks described here are specific to forced-air heating systems and are jobs that can be undertaken by the average do-it-yourselfer with the help of the furnace manufacturer's manual for the home-owner.

Lubricate the fan motor twice a year, once at the beginning of the heating season and once midway through the season, or as recommended by the manufacturer. At the same time, lubricate any other motor or bearing in the system. Flush mineral deposits from the humidifier twice a year.

Once a year, vacuum all exposed, accessible surfaces in and around the furnace, particularly within the blower compartment and burner. Have your furnace professionally serviced every year before the start of the heating season. Many utility companies provide this service for their customers.

Replace disposable air filters, or clean washable and electrostatic filter plates, every month. Examine the registers periodically for dark stains.

Steam Heat

As the name implies, steam is the medium by which heat is distributed through the house. An oil- or gas-fired burner heats water in the boiler until it becomes steam (see figure 9.2). The hot steam rises through pipes that bring it to radiators in each room. After the steam gives up its heat, it cools and condenses into water again. This water, known as condensate, returns by the force of gravity to the boiler, where it is recycled into steam.

Steam heating may use a single pipe system, in which the steam rises and the condensate falls through the same pipe; or a two-pipe system, in which steam rises through one pipe and condensate falls through another. Most private homes with steam heat have single-pipe systems. Radiators must be tilted so that the condensate does not accumulate and block the pipe. Each radiator must be equipped with a valve called an air vent that permits air to escape from the radiator, allowing steam to enter. If an air valve is blocked or closed, no steam will be able to enter the radiator, and it will not get hot. Additional air vents called quick vents are usually installed on branch circuits of the system to allow air to escape.

Many large houses with two-pipe steam systems use *steam traps* instead of air vents. A steam trap is a thermostatically controlled device located in each

radiator at the return pipe. The steam trap closes and blocks off the return pipe when it senses the hot steam. The steam can then fill the radiator. When the steam condenses, the cooler water lowers the temperature at the trap, and the trap opens. The water returns to the boiler, and the radiator can vent itself through the return system.

There are several devices on a steam boiler that control its operation. One such safety device is the low-water cutoff. Since some water is lost from a steam system through unnoticeable leaks and air vents, it is important for the homeowner to check and replenish the water supply, as needed, at least once a week—twice a week is preferable—during the heating season. (The boiler will have a sight glass, a gauge that shows the water level.) If this is not done, or if there is a large loss of water for some other reason, the low-water cutoff prevents the boiler from firing and seriously damaging itself, possibly beyond repair. It is also imperative that water be drained until it runs clear from the low-water cutoff once a month during the heating season, and that the boiler be refilled with clean water.

Many steam boilers also have an automatic water feed, either as part of the low-water cutoff or as a separate unit. This monitors the water level in the boiler and adds water to the system when it drops below a preset level. Although this feature eliminates the need to fill the boiler by hand, the homeowner must still check the boiler's water level to make certain the water feed is working.

An aquastat, a thermostat that senses water temperature, triggers the boiler periodically, even when the room thermostat is not calling for heat, in order to keep the boiler water hot. An aquastat is installed when the boiler is used to provide hot tap water, which is kept hot by passing through a coil of pipe or tubing that is submerged in the boiler water. There must be no mixing of boiler water and hot tap water. Boiler water picks up corrosion from radiators, pipes, and the boiler itself, and it is unfit for domestic use. In addition, boiler water frequently contains poisonous chemical additives that inhibit rust.

Once the thermostat signals for heat, the boiler fires until the minimum room temperature reaches that set on the thermostat. This could keep the boiler firing all day in frigid weather, and pressure in the boiler would become excessive. For this rea-

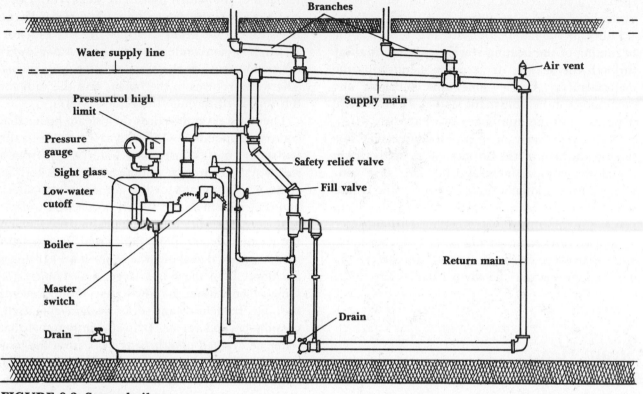

FIGURE 9.2 Steam boiler

son, a device known as a pressurtrol is attached to the steam boiler. The pressurtrol shuts down the boiler once a preset pressure is reached, usually about ¾ to 1½ pounds per square inch (psi). When the pressure drops by another preset amount, usually ½ to 1 psi, the boiler is again allowed to fire until the preset pressure is reached again.

The pressurtrol is an operating control as opposed to a safety device. It is expected to shut down and turn on the boiler firing mechanism during normal operation of the system. The relief valve, on the other hand, is a safety mechanism that allows hot steam to blow off into the boiler room when the pressure becomes excessive and threatens safety, usually between 12 and 15 psi. This mechanism is *not* expected to be triggered during normal operation of the steam boiler. A relief valve is needed in case the pressurtrol fails.

Sometimes found in steam boilers in private homes, and required in certain parts of the United States for steam systems in multiple-family dwellings, the manually resettable pressurtrol is a cross between a high-pressure relief valve and a pres-

surtrol. The pressure setting on a manually resettable pressurtrol is higher than that for the regular pressurtrol, but much lower than the setting for a safety relief valve. Still, this pressure should not be reached during the normal operation. If it is, something is wrong with the system and this device shuts it down. The resettable pressurtrol prevents the boiler from firing again until the reset button is pushed. The reset button is usually red and appears only on the resettable pressurtrol; otherwise the two types of pressurtrols look very much alike. The purpose of the reset button is to get the attention of the homeowner or superintendent responsible for the operation of the system. Do not simply reset it and forget it. Call in professional help.

Inspection and Maintenance

Conduct an inspection of your steam heating system at the start of and midway through the heating season.

Turn off the power to the boiler, and locate the sight glass. Check the level of water in the boiler, and fill the boiler as necessary. Once the water is up to its proper level, fire up the boiler by setting the house thermostat to a temperature higher than that in the room in which it is located. The boiler should fire and continue to run. With the boiler running and a bucket placed under the low-water cutoff cleanout, open the cleanout (or blow-off) valve and let some water run into the bucket. The boiler should shut down automatically as water runs out the cleanout. If the boiler does not shut off, the low-water cutoff is not working properly. In that case, fill the boiler to the correct level, and call a heating contractor to repair or replace the device.

While the system is working, monitor the water level over several days. If you note an excessive loss of water, as compared with your previous experience with the boiler, search for leakage. Water can leak from a cracked pipe, a defective air vent, a shut-off valve, or, in the worst case, a cracked boiler. Usually a cracked boiler will flood the basement, and the loss of water will shut down the system. But a boiler that is losing water does not always leave telltale puddles nearby. Sometimes the boiler leaks into the burner, and the leaking water evaporates and goes up the chimney. If this is the case, the only way to determine whether the boiler is leaking is to give it a pressure test, a job that must be left to a professional heating contractor.

You may find that the water level in the boiler is rising rather than staying the same or falling. It may be that a hole or crack in the hot tap-water coil, if you have one, is allowing water to pass out of the coil into the boiler water. If so, the coil needs replacement. Another possible cause of rising water level is a defective automatic-fill valve. In either case, call a professional heating contractor.

Look for smoke stains around the boiler wherever there is a joint or seam. This may indicate puff backs caused by late ignition, calling for an adjustment of the oil gun by a professional.

After inspecting the boiler itself, go from room to room checking the radiators and looking for problems. If you find one or more radiators that do not heat up when others on the same floor do, there is a good chance that the air vents on the cold radiators are broken. To replace an air vent, turn off the heating system, unscrew the defective vent, and take it to your hardware or plumbing-supply store so that you can purchase an effective replacement. Simply screw the new part into the same radiator. Air vents differ in how readily they release air out of the radiator—they operate at different pressures. Lower numbers (1, 2, 3, 4) or letters earlier in the alphabet (A, B, C, D) normally indicate a lower pressure rating, which means the vent will work and the radiator heat up more quickly. If you want the radiator to heat up faster, a vent with a lower number or an earlier-in-the-alphabet letter should be used to replace the existing one.

Another reason for a cold or cool radiator is a defective shut-off valve or one that is simply turned off. Shut-off valves are usually right-hand valves and close down if turned clockwise; they turn on when rotated counterclockwise. If opening the shut-off valve completely doesn't cause the radiator to function, the valve may be defective. Replacement of a radiator shut-off valve should be done by a plumber or heating contractor.

Once a month during the heating season, shut off the power to the boiler, drain off the low-water cutoff until the water runs clear, and fill the boiler to the appropriate level. Lubricate all motors in the system twice a year, once at the beginning of and again midway into the heating season. Replace air valves when they get noisy or when a radiator refuses to heat up. Never paint air valves.

Dealing with Problems

If during the heating season your steam system shuts down, there are a few things to check before calling a service person:

- Check to see that the power switch has not been inadvertently shut off.
- Check the circuit breaker or fuse protecting the

circuit to the boiler. Replace the fuse if it's blown, or reset the circuit breaker.

- Examine the sight glass to determine whether there is adequate water in the boiler. This is a common cause for shutdown.
- Press the reset button. Do this only once; more often will tend to flood the boiler with fuel.
- Check the thermostat. Turn the setting down and then up to see if the unit goes on. It may be that the contacts on the thermostat are dirty. Wipe the contacts with a clean piece of rough paper from a brown paper bag. Do not disturb other elements of the thermostat as you do this.

If the above steps don't restore the system to normal operation, call a professional.

Hot-Water Heating

In this type of system the medium for the transfer of heat is water (see figure 9.3). The water is not boiled and turned into steam, but heated to a maximum temperature of about 200 degrees F. One of the advantages of the hot-water system is that the water can be circulated at a temperature well below the maximum if it is not very cold outside. The circulating water temperature can be in the 90 to 100 degree range and provide sufficient warmth at less cost and without very hot radiators.

When the thermostat signals for heat in the circulating hot-water system, the boiler fires and a pump called the circulator turns on. Water circulates through the system as it increases in temperature, warming radiators, baseboard units, or, in the case of radiant heat, coils embedded in the floor or ceiling. If the boiler is designed to fire when triggered by the thermostat, it is called a "demand operation."

If the boiler is also used for heating household water, a minimum boiler temperature must be maintained continuously, even when the thermostat is not calling for heat.

Devices that measure the temperature of boiler and circulating water are called aquastats, and are either low-limit or high-limit switches, depending on their function. Low-limit switches turn on and high-limit switches turn off the system.

Most boilers in hot-water systems are equipped with an automatic fill mechanism that adds water to the system when the pressure drops below a preset value, usually about 12 psi for single- or two-story homes. Frequently a combination regulator/relief valve is used. The regulator allows fresh water to enter when the system pressure drops below the 12 psi limit, and the relief valve allows water to drain out when the pressure exceeds the upper limit, usually 30 psi. The relief valve is a safety device; pressure should not exceed 30 psi during normal operation. If the relief valve is allowing water to drain, something is wrong in the system.

A common cause of excessive pressure is a waterlogged expansion tank. Water cannot be compressed, and its volume increases greatly as it is heated; therefore pressure increases greatly when water is heated within a confined space. The expansion tank is included in the system to allow water to increase in volume without creating excessive pressure. (The expansion bottle attached to your car's radiator works the same way.) There are two types of expansion tanks used with hot-water heating systems. One is a bladder type that can be serviced only by a professional. It usually requires very little, if any, maintenance. The other is a plain empty tank, which needs to be bled of excess water annually. The homeowner can do this by closing the isolation valve, which shuts the tank off from the system, and opening the drain valve. Water emptying from the tank should be directed either to a large bucket or by hose to a sink. Continue until the tank is empty. Then close the drain valve and open the isolation valve so the system will again function.

A common distribution system for hot-water heating is the single-pipe series loop. Hot water leaves the boiler and moves in one continuous line through each radiator or baseboard unit in succession, eventually returning to the boiler. The main difficulty with this arrangement is that no one radiator can be turned off individually, since doing so would stop circulation in the entire system. For this reason, some single-pipe loop systems have branch pipes that individually connect each radiator or baseboard unit to the main supply line. If

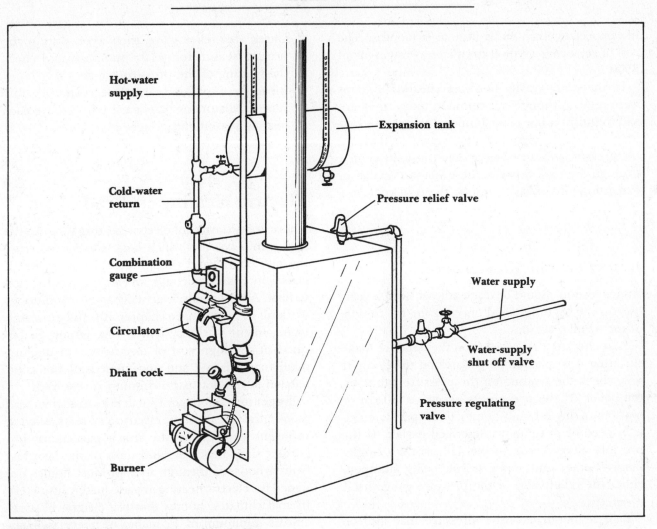

FIGURE 9.3 Circulating hot-water boiler

one unit is shut down, the hot water simply bypasses it.

Another configuration, the two-pipe system, has one line that supplies the hot water and another that brings the cooled water back to the boiler to be reheated. Radiators and baseboard units, equipped with shut-off valves, are individually connected to each of these two pipes, allowing for any unit to be turned off without affecting the others. This type of system requires the periodic bleeding of each of the radiators or baseboard units. To bleed a radiator means to open its bleeder valve and release trapped air. The bleeder valves are operated either by a screwdriver or by a special key that can be purchased at most hardware stores. With the circulator running, the bleeder valve is kept open until all the trapped air is released and

a steady stream of water begins to come from the valve. Be sure to have a cup ready to catch the water before opening the valve. The valve is then shut.

A circulating hot-water heating system can be easily "zoned," allowing for separate areas of the home, or zones, to be heated independently. Each zone has its own thermostat, and an electrically operated valve on its supply line. Whenever a thermostat demands heat, the valve to that zone opens and the circulator pushes hot water through it. In some zoned systems, usually in larger homes, each zone has its own circulator.

The motors of the circulators must be oiled at least once and preferably twice a year with electric motor oil. With proper lubrication, a circulator should last 25 years. But if left unlubricated, the life expectancy can be as little as 6 months. The cost of replacing a typical circulator averages about $500.

In the past, gravity hot-water heating systems were used. Although not common today, they are still found in a few older homes. In a gravity hot-water system the circulator and expansion tank are not present, and the water system is usually vented through the roof. Some of these systems do use an expansion tank, placed close to the roof vent.

Inspection and Maintenance

An inspection should be done at least twice a year, once at the beginning and once during the middle of the heating season.

First check the relief valve on the boiler to make sure that it is not dumping water on the floor. If it is, check the reading on the pressure gauge on the boiler. If the pressure is excessive (30 psi or more for a single-family home), the expansion tank is in need of purging, as described earlier. If the pressure gauge reads normal (12 psi for a single-family home) and water is still being dumped, either the relief valve or the pressure gauge itself is defective.

Bear in mind, excessive pressure may also be caused by a damaged hot-water coil in a boiler that produces household hot water as well as heat. If the coil develops a leak, water from the main supply system will leak into the boiler water. A faulty pressure-reducing valve on the automatic feed can also cause excessive boiler pressure.

If you notice that the circulator is noisy, try some lubricating oil. If this doesn't work, have it serviced by a heating contractor.

You should regularly carry out a few procedures to maintain your system. Shut off electric power to the heating system before doing the following maintenance work:

- As mentioned, lubricate the circulator and motors twice a year, once at the beginning of and once midway through the heating season.
- Drain water from nonbladder type expansion tanks at the beginning of each heating season.

- Check the relief valve each week during the heating season for water dumping, and check the reading of the pressure gauge.
- Bleed the expansion tank if necessary.
- Bleed radiators or baseboard units before each heating season and as needed.

Electric Heating in Brief

There are two types of electric heating systems: the heat pump type, in which heat is extracted from the outside air, and the resistance type, in which electricity passing through an element is converted to heat. A heat pump is actually an air conditioner working in reverse (see chapter 10). In both cases, management of the system is very important because of the high cost of electricity. Fortunately, maintenance is low, and since there is no fuel combustion in the house, no chimney is required.

Proper insulation is critical to the satisfactory and economical operation of electrical systems. Having sufficient insulation in the attic is particularly important since heat rises and most of the heat loss from a house is through its top. Most homes designed for electric heating are adequately insulated. In cold climates, homes that use electric heat require a minimum of 12 inches of fiberglass insulation in the floor of the attic. (Homes warmed by nonelectric heating systems require a minimum of 6 inches of such insulation.) Frequently foamboard insulation is placed around the foundation of a building when electric heat is to be used. In some cases, additional panels of insulation are placed on the exterior walls before installing the exterior siding.

Resistance heating usually employs either baseboard panels secured to the wall, each containing its own heating element, or electric "radiant" heating panels in the ceilings. The only maintenance required with this type of system is periodic vacuuming of the baseboard units to keep them dust-free.

Staying Warm

No matter what type of heating system is in your home, it is critical to your comfort that it be in good operating condition. The information presented here should serve you well by helping you stay warm during the winter.

When the weather does finally warm up, your objective will be the reverse: to cool your home. The next chapter, on air conditioning, will help you accomplish this goal.

10

AIR CONDITIONING

There are three commonly used methods of artificially cooling homes. Your house may have been constructed with a central air-conditioning system, powered either by electricity or by natural gas, or you may simply have window air-conditioning units, powered by electricity. Some houses, principally in the South and Southwest, use the technique of evaporative cooling, which uses your household water supply.

Electric and Gas Central Air Conditioning

A central air-conditioning system normally has four basic components: the blower, or fan; the evaporator coil; the condenser unit, consisting of a compressor pump and a condensing coil and fan; and the ductwork and vents.

The blower, not visible unless you remove its housing cover, is a device shaped like a squirrel cage with blades that make it resemble the paddle wheel on an old riverboat. Its function is to push air through the system. In most centrally air-conditioned homes the cooling and heating systems are combined, so that air from the blower passes through the furnace unit. When the furnace is off

during the summer, the heating system does not interfere with the cooling system. However, if your house has hot-water or steam heating, the blower and evaporator coil will be separated from the boiler.

The arrangement of components in this system can vary. If the components are stacked vertically in a basement or closet with the blower on the bottom of the stack, below the furnace, the fan is blowing air up through the furnace in what is known as an upflow system. If the blower is above the furnace, the reverse is true, making it a downflow system. If the components are placed in an attic or crawl space, the arrangement may be horizontal, with the blower on the side of the furnace. If you're in doubt about the direction of flow, feel around the registers when the air conditioning is on. Cold air emerges from the ducts attached to the evaporator coil.

The important thing to remember about the blower is that this is where the filter is usually located. Your system may have filters behind the return-air vents in the rooms of the house, or inside the return-air plenum, but a filter at the blower is the most common arrangement. You may have to unscrew and remove a cover to get at the filter. Its purpose is to clean the air before it passes through the blower, and it is probably the single most important maintenance item in the entire system. Check your filter every month, and clean or replace it as often as suggested by the manufacturer.

How the System Works

The operation of air conditioners, or refrigeration equipment for that matter, is based on the behavior of refrigerant and its ability to absorb and give off heat. The evaporator coil and the condenser unit of an air-conditioning system are designed to exploit this behavior to remove heat from the air circulating in your house, carry it out of the house, and dispel the heat outside.

A refrigerant circulates in a closed system from the compressor to the condenser coil to the evaporator coil and back to the compressor (see figure 10.1). The compressor, condenser coil, and a fan are located outside the house. The condenser coil may resemble a car radiator, or the design may be a coiled tube with fins on it. The evaporator coil is located inside the house, within the flow of circulating air, downwind of the blower. When one coil (the evaporator) removes heat from room air and the other coil (the condenser) transfers the heat to the outside of the house, cooling takes place.

The compressor pumps high pressure, hot refrigerant gas into the condenser coil, where a fan cools it and it gives up its heat to the outside air. The gas cools into a liquid and is pushed under high pressure to the evaporator coil, where it sprays into the coil through an expansion device, becoming a cool gas in the process. As this cool refrigerant, now under low pressure, moves through the evaporator coil, it absorbs heat from the air flowing around it and cools that air. The refrigerant then returns to the compressor, and the process repeats itself. The circulating refrigerant and circulating house air are two entirely separate systems—no refrigerant should mix with air—only heat passes from one system to the other.

When the air-conditioning unit is running during the summer months, the evaporator coil should get *very* cold, so cold that it "sweats," that is, it collects condensing moisture from the circulating air. Water dripping off an evaporator coil is collected in a pan and piped to a drain. However, if you have

a horizontal flow unit in your attic, it should be equipped with a secondary condensation drain (see chapter 2). Sooner or later the primary drain will clog up with airborne dust or algae growth, and the secondary drain will prevent an overflow of water into the ceiling below. The pipe from the secondary drain pan should run through the eaves to the outside of the house somewhere near a front or rear door. This way you are more likely to notice water flowing from the secondary drain, a clear warning that the primary drain is clogged.

Except for reversible heat pump systems (see below), your air-conditioning system should not be operated when the outside air temperature is below about 60 degrees F. At colder temperatures the refrigerant gas, under high pressure, will condense to a liquid inside the compressor, and this may damage the pump.

Heat Pumps

A variation on the basic central air-conditioning system is the heat pump. This system combines household cooling and heating by means of a reversible switching valve. In the summer the heat pump system works like conventional central air conditioning, but in the winter the function of the two coils can be reversed. Gas in the coil outside the house now absorbs heat from the outside air, and the coil inside the household air flow now transfers heat to that air. As mentioned in Chapter 9, it is air conditioning in reverse.

Natural Gas

Electric central air-conditioning systems work as described above, with electricity powering the blower and compressor pump to make the system go. Central air-conditioning systems powered by natural gas have many of the same components as electric systems—blowers, filters, an evaporator coil, a condenser coil, ductwork—but the gas system has no electrically operated compressor pump. Instead, a gas flame is used to heat and raise the pressure of a refrigerant and drive it through the

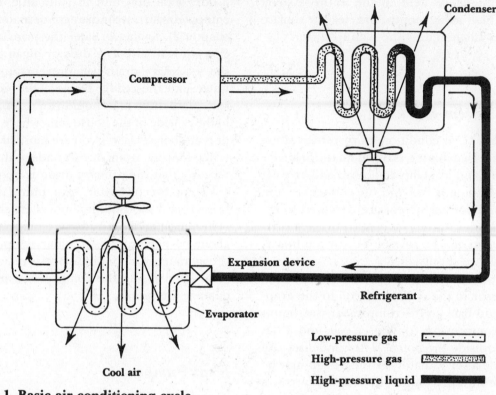

Condenser

Compressor

Expansion device

Refrigerant

Evaporator

Cool air

Low-pressure gas

High-pressure gas

High-pressure liquid

FIGURE 10.1 Basic air-conditioning cycle

system. In addition, the refrigerant is not a gas, but ammonia.

The evaporator coil is designed a little differently as well. It is outside the house. It is surrounded by another manifold containing a water-antifreeze mixture. This unit, insulated in styrofoam, is called the heat exchanger. The ammonia draws heat from the water-antifreeze mix, which runs to a cooling coil inside the house blower and ductwork system. It is this separate cooling coil that conditions the air.

Measuring Performance

The ability of an air-conditioning system to remove heat energy from a home is most commonly stated in British Thermal Units, or BTUs. Occasionally you may see the term *Ton* used; there are about 12,000 BTUs in a Ton. Often not stated, but always implied, is that the BTU rating is the amount of heat transferred per hour.

A single BTU might best be described as a small but appreciable amount of heat energy. It takes one BTU of heat to raise the temperature of 1 pound of water—about two drinking glasses full—1 degree F. You can readily see why air-conditioner ratings are in the thousands of BTUs.

It takes a system with a capacity of approximately 12,000 BTUs to cool a space of about 4,800 cubic feet. That represents a floor area of about 20 by 30 feet, about the size of a two-car garage, with a ceiling height of 8 feet. It would take a capacity of about 36,000 BTUs to cool an average house of about 1,800 square feet of floor space, with average insulation and windows. If you live in a contemporary home with 20-foot-high vaulted ceilings, large picture windows, and lots of frequently used doors, your home may need twice as many BTUs as an average homeowner's.

The two heat-exchanging elements of your system, the evaporator coil and the condenser unit, must have compatible BTU capacities. And the system as a whole should not be more powerful than necessary. This can cause the evaporator coil to freeze, resulting in compressor damage, or the unit may cycle on and off too frequently, using excessive energy and failing to operate long enough to effectively reduce humidity.

The Ductwork

Ductwork carries your house air to and from the heating and cooling units. The return-air ductwork routes the air from the house to the blower so that it may be recooled and carried through the supply-air ductwork to the various rooms.

There is normally a box right next to the blower unit called the return-air plenum. All the air from the return-air ductwork is gathered in the plenum and fed back through the system to be cooled. If the return-air ducts and the return-air plenum are *in* the air-conditioned area of the house, they need not be insulated. If these components are not within an air-conditioned area, that is, if they are in the attic or under the house in a crawl space, the ducts should be insulated to make the system more efficient. In addition, all ductwork seams in spaces that are not air conditioned should be well sealed with duct tape.

The supply-air ductwork should always be insulated in spaces that are not air conditioned so that it can deliver the coldest air possible to the rooms. If the ducts are in a damp area like the attic or basement, they could sweat and cause water damage if not insulated (see chapter 2). Dampness could also rust metal ductwork, or cause mildew and fungus to grow inside the duct.

Each room's supply register should have an *adjustable* grille whether it's located on the wall, the ceiling, or the floor. You should be able to adjust the cover from fully open to fully closed. Adjusting the registers is important to your comfort and pocketbook. If one room in your house is too cold and the other is too hot, simply adjust the registers to put the cool air where you need it. If you have a spare room that is hardly ever used, close the register to increase the flow of cool air to rooms that are in use; close the door to the unused room.

The supply air must have a path back to the return-air plenum so that air can circulate properly. If a particular room doesn't have a return-air vent, and you close the door, you might reduce the flow of cool air to that room. One simple way to solve this problem is to cut about ¾ to 1 inch off the bottom of the door. Room air can then get out into the hallway and return to the central system. This solution can diminish the room's privacy, however, for more sound will carry through the door opening than before.

Window Units

A window air-conditioning unit has all the same parts as a central system, but they're much smaller, of course, and they are packed into one box case. The box case is normally divided into two compartments separated by a metal or cardboard wall. The inside compartment, the one nearest the room, contains the blower and evaporator coil. The outside compartment contains the compressor, condenser coil, and condenser fan. There must be a filter in the inside compartment to clean the air before it passes through the blower. The filter is very important. It is usually behind the decorative front cover. If your unit lacks a filter, get one.

A window unit is installed in the frame of a window or occasionally in an opening cut in the wall. The unit should be well sealed around the edges to prevent outside air from entering the home.

When installing a window unit, never twist or cut the prongs of the electrical cord to force them to fit into the receptacle. Many kinds of plugs are used on window units. Some are for 220 volts; others are for 110 volts. Before installation, read the data plate on the machine and check the voltage rating of your receptacle or circuit. If you are in doubt, call an electrician. An improper electrical connection may damage the unit or cause an electrical fire.

On window units, water dripping off the evaporator coil collects in a pan and is piped to the outside compartment. This water can be disposed of in two ways. It may simply drip onto the ground outside, or it can be blown out as a vapor by the condenser fan. In the latter case, the fan has a small scoop called a slinger that picks up a small amount of water as the fan spins and blows it out through the condenser coil.

There should be no obstructions to air flow in

front of the window unit. If the blower sucks in a curtain, for example, the air flow can be choked off and the unit can be damaged. Conversely, if cold air is bouncing off the back of a chair and back into the unit, the unit's thermostat can be fooled into thinking the room is cold and it will shut off the compressor.

Evaporative Coolers

Evaporative coolers operate by passing air through a wet material. As air passes through, water evaporates, forming a cool vapor that is blown into the house. This system is most efficient in dry climates and is usually used to cool homes in desert areas, although some homes in the humid southern states use them. Evaporative coolers are also employed to cool and humidify greenhouses.

The typical evaporative system has six basic parts: float-actuated water valve, water pan, water pump and hose, water tray, fiber evaporative material, and blower.

The float-actuated valve assembly is connected to a cold-water pipe. It is very similar to the float-and-valve assembly used to fill a traditional toilet tank. The float rises with the water level in the water pan and forces the valve shut when the pan is full. When the water level drops, the float falls and opens the valve, and water fills the pan. The water pump and hose sit in the water pan. The water pump pushes water up through the hose into the water tray. This tray has numerous small holes in its bottom through which water trickles out and wets a sheet of fibrous material. The blower draws outside air through the wet fiber material, the moisture evaporates, and cool air is blown into the home.

Making Sure You Stay Cool

It is advisable to inspect your central air-conditioning system, window unit, or evaporative cooler at least twice a year, once at the beginning of the cooling season and again during the cooling season.

You will need a flashlight, a thermometer, a screwdriver, a 1-foot-long piece of yarn, tissue paper, and a pen and paper. Make written notes of any problems you find to help you organize your maintenance tasks later. Always shut off electricity to the system before poking around near motors, blowers, fans, drive belts, or other moving parts.

Central Air Conditioning

On a day when the outside temperature is above 65 degrees F, start inside the house at the thermostat. Turn the fan switch to "automatic" and turn the control switch on the thermostat to "cool." Set the thermostat at 65 degrees F.

INSIDE THE HOUSE

To see if there is a good air flow coming from the room registers take a 1-foot-long piece of yarn and hold it in front of each one. The breeze should be strong enough to make the yarn flutter. The registers should be adjusted for proper air flow as needed for comfort and energy saving. In a two-story house with one central system, most of the cold air should be directed to the second floor supply registers (outlets). Since heat rises and most of the heat energy strikes the roof, sending more cool air to the upstairs rooms will compensate for those effects. It will also create cooler bedrooms, which are desirable for comfortable sleeping in the summer. Because cool air falls, gravity will bring some of the air to cool the downstairs rooms, thus compensating for the lower flow to them.

Check the return-air vents by placing a tissue over the return registers. If the draw is good, the tissue will adhere to the grilles.

Go to the furnace and check the cover to the blower compartment; it should be secure so that air cannot be sucked in from the furnace area. Listen for a hissing or whistling noise that would indicate the blower cover is not fitted properly. The blower cover should *never* be off when the system is operating; call for service if it is.

Shut off the electrical power to the system and remove the cover. Check the blower compartment to locate the filter. If you don't find it there, it will probably be behind a louvered grille nearby. Using a flashlight, check to see if the filter is clean. If not, wash it, or replace it if it's a replaceable filter. Washable filters are usually made of a stiff horsehair-type or metal fiber. They should be washed in detergent water, then dried and sprayed with a dust collector of the type used on a dust mop. Replaceable filters are made of thin fiberglass in a cardboard frame. When inserting such filters, be sure the air-flow arrow printed on the edge of the cardboard frame is pointing toward the blower area.

While you have the blower compartment open, look at the blades on the blower with a flashlight. They should be fairly clean. A thin layer of dust is acceptable, but not a thick coating. If the blades need cleaning, call a service company; cleaning a blower is a surprisingly dirty job.

While you're in the furnace area, look for the air-conditioning condensation drain. It's usually a ¾ inch plastic or copper pipe coming out of the bottom of the evaporator coil, and it leads to a drain. The condensation drain should not be overflowing into the furnace or on the floor. If it is overflowing, call an air-conditioning specialist. As discussed earlier, attic systems should have a secondary condensation drain.

Replace the cover, turn the air conditioner on, and let it run about 5 minutes. With your hand, see if you can feel a cold breeze coming from any area of the ductwork. If the seams in the ducts are not sealed properly, air can escape and lessen the efficiency of your system. Loosely fitted seams can be taped with duct tape. Supply-air ducts should be insulated.

A properly functioning system reduces the temperature of the incoming air 15 to 20 degrees F as it passes through the evaporator coil. Place a thermometer in the blower compartment or tape it to the return-air grille for about 5 minutes and take a reading. Now place the thermometer in the supply register nearest to the cooling unit for 5 minutes and take another reading. You should note a 15- to 20-degree difference. Expect smaller temperature drops in humid weather or if the system has long duct runs.

THE CONDENSER

If the condenser coil is outside, it should be kept clean to "blow off" the excess heat most efficiently. Check to see that no vines, plastic covers, or anything else such as tall grass or shrubbery obstructs the air flow. If you find any obstructions, clear them away. Two refrigerant lines usually come out of the condenser unit in the same location, near the ground. The pencil-sized copper pipe coming out of the condenser unit and running back to the evaporator should never be hot to the touch, but just about 20 degrees above the outside temperature. If the line is hot to the touch, the condenser coil may be dirty. You can look at the coil with a flashlight. It should be visible behind the louvers on the exterior of the case. If the fins on the coil appear to be dirty, shut off the electricity to the condenser unit and wash the coil with high-pressure water from a garden hose. Be sure to spray the water through the coil from the side opposite the dirty side so that the dirt will be washed out of the coil and not forced deeper into it.

With the system on, check the suction line. The suction line is the tube that carries refrigerant gas to the condenser unit. It is about the diameter of a hotdog and should be insulated with foam rubber. The suction line should be cold, like a glass of ice water, never warm and never frozen. If the line insulation is badly deteriorated or missing, you can buy replacement insulation at most hardware stores.

The condenser unit should be sitting on a level platform, usually a concrete slab. It doesn't have to be perfectly level, but if the unit is obviously tilted, it should be adjusted or else the compressor can be damaged. It's best to have a professional make this adjustment. You could bend the refrigerant lines while moving the unit; the bent pipes could restrict the refrigerant flow and damage the compressor.

The high-voltage and low-voltage wires usually enter the condenser housing on one side near the top. Check to see if the high-voltage wires to the condenser unit are protected by metal conduit so that there is no chance of electrical shock. Any splices or bare-wire connections in the low-voltage wiring should be wrapped with electrical tape or connected with wire nuts so that they can't create a short. (This bundle of small multicolored wires is usually encased in a brown plastic wrapper. Wire nuts look like the caps on tubes of toothpaste.) The low-voltage wires come from the thermostat in the house. They carry signals to the control devices in the condenser unit and turn the compressor on and off. Any repairs needed should be done by a professional.

Turn the air conditioner off after you complete your inspection, unless it's needed for comfort. If in the course of your inspection you find good air flow from each supply vent, a temperature drop of 15 to 20 degrees F, a suction line as cold as ice water, and the liquid line not hot to the touch, your home's central cooling system is operating satisfactorily. If this is not the case, call for service by an air-conditioning specialist.

NATURAL GAS/AMMONIA SYSTEMS

In residential construction, natural gas and ammonia systems are relatively rare. Nevertheless, for homes that have them, most of the inspections are exactly the same as for electric and gas-refrigerant systems. You can check the supply and return registers and filters, and make certain the air blowing into the house is cooler than the air returning to the evaporator coil. You can make sure the condenser unit is unobstructed, clean, and level, and that no wire connections to the condenser cooling fan are exposed. But it is extremely difficult for an inexperienced person to differentiate between and check the relative temperature of the two sets of pipes leading to and from the evaporator (water and antifreeze) and the condenser (ammonia). Temperature checks are best left to a professional.

Window Units

Inspect the window unit when the temperature is above 65 degrees F, but before using the unit for the first time in the air-conditioning season, go outside and make sure that there is adequate breathing room around it. No vines or other obstructions

should be wrapped around the outside case. Remove plastic covers. Make sure that all the seams around the case are sealed to keep outside air from entering the house. Use exterior caulking as needed.

Go back into the house and remove the decorative front cover of the unit. This can usually be done by removing two screws on the side, or you may have to push down (or up) and pull out on the bottom of the cover to remove it. There should be a filter behind the front cover. Follow the instructions given earlier for washing or replacing it.

Turn on the unit, and allow it to operate for 5 minutes. There should be good air flow from the front cover, enough to make a length of yarn flutter. Turn off the unit and examine the exposed tubing on the sides of the evaporator coil, which should be cold and sweaty, like a glass of ice water. You may have to pull the unit into the room a few inches in order to see the sides of the coil. The coil should not be frozen or warm. If the coil is not at the proper temperature, call for service.

Unplug the electrical cord from the wall, and look at the blower with a flashlight. The fins on the blower should be clean. If they are caked with dust, call for service.

As mentioned, make sure there are no obstructions to air flow in front of the window unit. If the blower "sucks in" a curtain, the air flow can be choked off and the unit can freeze up. If the cold air is bounced back into the unit, the thermostat will not control the unit properly.

Replace the filter and cover. The temperature drop across the evaporator coil should be in the range of 15 to 20 degrees F. The intake grille can be located with a piece of tissue, which will be sucked against the front cover at the intake. Tape your thermometer to the intake grille (at side of the front decorative cover) and plug the unit in, turn it on, and let it run for about 5 minutes. Take a reading. Now place the thermometer at the outlet grille for about 5 minutes with the unit still running. Measure the difference. Expect to have smaller temperature drops in humid weather.

Evaporative Coolers

Evaporator coolers are simple machines, and therefore they are relatively trouble-free. To check one, first go outside and determine whether the vent to the blower has adequate breathing room; remove any obstructions.

Turn off the power to the cooler, and remove the outside metal cover plate. (Normally there are four screws near the bottom of the case that hold the cover in place.) Inspect the fiber material. Replace it if it is coated with minerals from the water or if the fiber is fragile when you touch it. In regions where coolers are used, new fiber material is usually available in home centers or hardware stores.

Pull the drain plug to drain the water pan. Let the pan drain, and clean out any debris in the water pan and water tray with a scraper and brush. Check the bottom of the water pump, and remove any dirt that may be blocking the water-intake holes. Make sure all the holes in the bottom of the water tray that drips on the fiber are open. You can use an ice pick or a nail to open the holes. If the bottom of the water pan or tray appears to be rusty, use a wire brush to remove the rust, and, when it is completely dry and clean, paint the bottom with a rust-resistant paint. Replace the drain plug in the bottom of the water pan, using an expandable rubber plug if the old plug is worn.

Check the blower drive belt as discussed later in this chapter. Clean and oil the blower, and replace the belt if necessary.

Turn on the water at the source. The float-valve assembly should fill the pan with water and shut off before the pan overflows. The water level should be below the height of the faucet spout inside the water pan to prevent backflow (see chapter 8). Bend the metal rod attached to the float to adjust the water level, but do not hold the float when bending the arm. The float is fragile and can be easily damaged.

Turn on the power switch; stay clear of moving pulleys and belts. The blower should be blowing air into the house. Check to see that the water pump is pushing water up to the water tray, and that water is dripping down on top of the fiber material. If the water pump is not working properly, check the specifications on the dataplate on the pump and

replace it, or have a repairperson replace it, with a pump of the same gallons-per-minute capacity. Water pumps are available at hardware stores, home centers, and plumbing-supply companies.

MOTORS, PULLEYS, AND BELTS

Central air conditioning and evaporative coolers have a variety of motors, pulleys, and belts that the homeowner can maintain. Shut off the electricity to all types of units before doing any work.

Check blower motors and condenser-fan motors to determine whether they have oil cups or oil holes. If so, oil the motors twice a year, at the start and middle of the cooling season, with 10 to 20 drops of electric motor oil. Many motors have plastic or metal caps in two small holes on the top outside edges of the motor if they require oil. Others have spring-loaded covers over the oil holes. Still others have sealed bearings and need no oil. Do not overoil, since this can harm the motor.

With belt-driven blowers (or belts used in gas air-conditioning pumps), check the tension on the belts; also check the inside edges of the belts for signs of cracking. Belts should be inspected at least twice each year, once at the beginning and once in the middle of the air-conditioning season. Replace the belts if necessary. When you push on them with moderate pressure, belts should have approximately ¾ to 1 inch of "play." If the belts are too tight, the bearings will wear out prematurely. On the other hand, a belt that's too loose provides inefficient power. The tension can be adjusted with a bolt near the motor.

Some Common Problems

Most problems with central or individual-unit air-conditioning systems make themselves apparent either through insufficient cooling or through leakage from the system. Some common problems, and the possible causes, follow.

It there's hardly any air coming out of the central air-conditioning vents, the problem might be that the filter hasn't been changed for many months and is clogged with dust. Simply change the filter. The blower belt might be loose or broken. In that case change the belt or adjust the tension.

The fins on the blower might be dirty. Dirty fins can't blow as much air as clean ones. If the blower is dirty, the evaporator coil is probably dirty too. Have them cleaned.

The evaporator coil might be frozen so that no air can pass through it. If the suction line at the condenser unit is frozen, the evaporator coil is frozen too. Shut off the air conditioning for a few hours until the coil defrosts. Check and clean the filter, blower, and evaporator coil. If everything's clean and the unit still freezes, you may be low on refrigerant. On the other hand, in an attempt to save energy, you may have closed too many registers, which can restrict the air flow through the system and cause the evaporator coil to freeze up. Some warm air flow over the coil is necessary to keep it defrosted. Open some registers. Call a service person if the evaporator continues to freeze.

If cooling is a problem in only one room, you may have a disconnected, damaged, or undersized duct. For a start, however, make certain that the room's register is open.

If you can hear the condenser unit operating outside and the blower is pushing air into the rooms but the air is not cool, your compressor may have developed a leak and become low on gas refrigerant. Shut the unit off, and call for service. Possibly one of the electrical devices—a relay or capacitor in the condenser unit—has failed, and the compressor can't start. The fan may be running even though the compressor is not. Or the compressor may simply have "died."

If water is dripping out of your air conditioner's evaporator coil box onto the floor, the pipe that carries the condensation from the coil to the drain is clogged, and the drain pan is overflowing. Remove the evaporator coil cover, clean out the drain pan, and unclog the drain pipe.

If the condenser unit outside keeps cycling on and off, you probably have a condenser unit with protective high-pressure and low-pressure cutoff switches. These switches sense abnormal refrigerant pressures and shut off the compressor to protect it from damage. Switches that cycle the air-conditioning system rapidly on and off usually indicate a dirty condenser coil, which is causing the unit to run hot with unusually high pressures. The compressor may also be low on refrigerant. Call for service.

If you detect water dripping out of your window unit onto the floor, the tube that carries the condensation from the drain pan in the inside compartment to the outside compartment may be clogged, causing the drain pan to overflow. Unplug the air conditioner, pull it out of the case, and look for the plastic tube that runs from the pan under the evaporator coil to the pan behind or under the outside condenser fan. Clean out the pans and tube, and reinstall the unit.

On the other hand, the entire unit may be tipped toward the room instead of toward the outside. Since water won't drain uphill, the drain pan will overflow into the house. Adjust the unit so that it slants slightly to the outside.

When considering repairs, never attempt to do them yourself unless you thoroughly understand the system. In any case, call in a professional whenever the problem involves wiring, checking refrigerant pressures, or replacing major components.

The following chapter will help you in your dealings with professionals, from hiring reputable people and setting up effective contracts to overseeing and paying for the repair work.

11

GETTING THE WORK DONE

Now that you've read at least some portions of this book, you may be seeing your house through new eyes. You can now appreciate the complexity of the systems in the home that are intended to keep you safe and comfortable. You probably have a better idea of what can go wrong with these systems and realize the importance of routine maintenance. But suppose something does go wrong, or that you decide to have repairs made after discovering problems in the course of your home inspection. Where do you go from here? Should you do the work yourself, or hire a professional?

Should You Do It Yourself?

All home repairs involve time, effort, and at least a little skill and knowledge. Only you can decide whether you are up to a particular project. Think first about the size and complexity of the work, and whether it involves more than one house system. From your reading you'll have some idea whether highly specialized skills are involved. If the work is extensive, complicated, requires special expertise, or must comply with local building codes, you are better off leaving the work to professionals.

If the task is one the average able-bodied person without special skills might accomplish, like cleaning out gutters, caulking, adding weather stripping, renailing boards, replacing sink washers, changing furnace filters, replacing a door-closer, grouting tile, and so on, go to the library or a bookstore for a book or video on the subject. Review all the stages of the project you will go through. Even if you are confident of your skills, most projects fare better with a few expert tips and the right tools. A good book will provide such information. Take note that every job is more complicated than it seems.

For anything beyond these simple repairs, you should also ask yourself whether you can do the work safely, particularly when electricity or moving machinery is involved. This doesn't just mean that you can complete the work without injuring yourself. You must not, through incompetent work, create a hazardous condition that will manifest itself later. Consider how long the job will take. If an afternoon or less, fine, but if it will take longer than a day, can the job be started and stopped without problems or inconvenience, and, considering the value of your own time, will it really cost you less to do it yourself?

Sometimes it makes sense to hire someone to do even simple maintenance tasks the first time. You can use this service call as an opportunity to learn. For example, when you have your furnace cleaned and serviced, watch where and how the filters go in. Ask the serviceperson how to perform other routine tasks.

Finding Others to Do the Work

If you've decided to hire a professional, of course you'll want someone who is competent, reliable, and whose services are reasonably priced. The more you know about the work, the better you'll be able to judge the tradesperson's statements. Use your friends, the Yellow Pages, and newspapers to find reliable firms from whom to request estimates. A favorable recommendation from a friend is the best reference; some would say it is the only reliable reference. If you notice a home or a building that looks well maintained or well repaired, ask the owner or manager who does the work. Lumberyards, building-supply houses, hardware stores, and tool-rental businesses may have bulletin boards filled with the business cards of local tradespeople, but you have no way of distinguishing the good from the bad.

The main thing for you to remember about bids and prices is to be precise and to work from a carefully prepared, written job description when asking for an estimate. If you are imprecise or leave out an important consideration for the tradesperson, differences in prices will be meaningless. Write down a rough set of specifications for the job you have in mind: List the work to be done, the kinds of materials you want used, and your budget for the project. Ask enough questions to satisfy yourself that you and the tradesperson understand each other. Get estimates from at least three professionals. Be suspicious of low bids.

Never go ahead with any project without making some careful checks. The contractor who did a wonderful job fixing your neighbor's siding may be on the verge of bankruptcy now. The photographs a carpenter shows you may not exhibit work the carpenter actually did.

Always ask the tradesperson for references and check them. Ask these individuals, as well as the person who might have recommended the professional in the first place, the following questions:

- Was the job done on time?
- Was the price within the limit quoted on the bid?
- Were they satisfied that the service was a fair value for the money?
- Would they hire this contractor again?

Check with the Better Business Bureau for any unresolved complaints about the tradesperson or company. An absence of complaints may only mean that the business is relatively new. A well-run business will resolve complaints taken to the Better Business Bureau; a string of complaints should be a red flag. If your community has licensing requirements, find out whether the tradesperson is licensed. Ask what professional organizations the person or company belongs to or is associated with. Both the National Association of Home Builders Remodeling Council and the National Association of the Remodeling Industry have membership requirements and codes of ethics to verify that the contractor is a member in good standing.

Before you hire anyone, check into the personal liability laws in your state. Find out what kind of coverage you have under your homeowner's insurance. This is especially important if the job involves working on a roof, being in a tree, or using power tools. If someone gets hurt while working for you, you may be liable for both medical payments and Worker's Compensation. To protect yourself, you may want to hire only people who carry their own insurance.

Agreements and Contracts

For minor repairs and maintenance under about $300, a handshake is usually the only agreement you have with your tradesperson, and this is normally adequate if you've carefully described the work you want done and checked out the person doing the work.

For work costing up to $1,000, ask at least for a written estimate before the work starts. The estimate should state what work will be done and how much it will cost. This is not as good as a contract, but it gives you some basis for argument if the final bill is much higher or the work is shoddy.

If the work is going to cost over $1,000, you definitely need a written agreement. You may want to consult a lawyer. Don't accept the contractor's version of the work contract—it's written primarily to protect the contractor, not you.

The contract should state the names and addresses of the parties involved. It should specify the itemized and total costs, and the start and completion dates. It should include a complete, precise description of the work to be done and the type and quality of materials. The payment schedule should be spelled out. It should state that the cost of all tools, labor, permits, and licenses is included in the price, that building codes will be complied with, that necessary inspections by local authorities will be done, and that the tradesperson or contractor accepts responsibility for negligent work. The homeowner should have the right to review and approve the work at various stages, and there should be a provision for negotiating work change orders. The tradesperson or contractor should promise to remove debris and leave the premises "broom clean." The work should be guaranteed for at least a year by written warranty in the contract.

Study the lien laws in your state and read the agreement carefully to see what the tradesperson or contractor can do to you or your property if you fail to pay him or her as expected. Be aware that if a person or company you've hired fails to pay suppliers, they can slap a lien (called a mechanic's or material man's lien) on your house. In effect, the lien gives suppliers the right to take your property, or some of it, as payment. The best way to protect yourself is to include a clause in the contract that states final payment wll not be made until a release of liens is delivered or receipts covering all labor, materials, and equipment are produced.

Paying for the Job

Never let the payments get ahead of the work. Whether you are dealing with a two-hour carpentry repair or a three-week remodeling job, the same principle applies. Make the final payment only upon satisfactory completion of the work and not before. Beware of a professional who pressures you

for money. As mentioned, the contract should have specific written terms for review of work and payment schedule.

You will probably have to pay a deposit, sometimes known as earnest or front money. Payment schedules differ depending on the locality, but expect to pay 10 to 20 percent earnest money before work begins and to make installment payments while the work is in progress. Never pay the final 15 to 25 percent until the work is completed to your satisfaction. Never sign a document that says the work has been completed until the work actually has been finished and you have inspected it carefully.

Try to get a clause in the contract stating that payment will be due 30 days after completion of the work—or even that payment will be withheld if the work slows down unreasonably. Called a hold-back clause, this gives you some leverage to get the work done on schedule and a chance to live with the work for a while and have defective work corrected before you make payment.

Work in Progress

When the work is finally under way, review its progress frequently. The person you've hired may even appreciate your interest. Since you've already learned something about the nature of the work before hiring anyone, you can see for yourself if you are getting what you asked for. With large, expensive jobs, it might be worthwhile to bring in another professional—an architect, engineer, or home inspector—to check the work against the plans and specifications. On projects that take more than a day, check over the work each evening. Raise any questions as soon as possible. Problems are always easier to fix when they are small. Be wary of a tradesperson or contractor who starts various sections of your project but never finishes any one of them. This can be a sign of things going seriously wrong. After the work is done, ask the person who performed the service to tell you exactly what was accomplished. Don't just assume everything has been done or that it has been done properly. Look the work over yourself and ask questions.

Winding Things Up

If your project involved several different contractors or a substantial amount of materials that the contractor supplied, ask for an affidavit of completion if it has not been offered. This affidavit is a notarized legal document. It states what work was to be done, and for how much money. Not all states require this affidavit, but it is desirable. Attached to the main affidavit, there should be other affidavits, the material man's affidavit, and the subcontractor's affidavit. There should be one for each person who provided materials or did work.

Disputes

Sometimes, especially with casual labor, a worker will walk off leaving the job unfinished. If you haven't paid for more work than has been completed—and you never should—write it off to experience and hire someone else to finish up.

If the work has been completed, however, at least in the professional's eye, but you are dissatisfied with the job for some reason, do not make the final payment and try to negotiate a settlement. You can ask to have changes made, or request a reduction in price. Be specific about what you want. It's easier to reach agreement on specifics than on generalities. It's better to say, "I want you to redo the left corner of the ceiling so it's smooth and flush" than to say, "the living room ceiling still isn't right."

If you can't reach a compromise and don't have a hold-back clause, and if you are holding up payment, the person you hired may take legal action. Don't ignore this possibility, since in many states anyone who has done work on your house can put a lien on it; typically you cannot sell a house that has a lien against it.

If you're determined not to pay for what you regard as inadequate work, you might consider asking a lawyer to send a letter stating what you want done and why you are not willing to pay. A letter from an attorney may encourage a settlement. Alternatively, get the other party to agree to binding arbitration and hire an arbiter, one or more independent people who will listen to both sides of the argument and recommend a fair settlement.

You can also file a complaint with your local Better Business Bureau, or file a suit in small-claims court if the sum of money involved is under the maximum allowed in your area. You can also file a suit in civil court if you and your lawyer believe you can prove incompetent work or significant damage to your property because of that work. Unfortunately, trying to solve repair and remodeling disputes in court may cost more than having the work done over. Try to avoid getting to this point by taking the time to find a reputable tradesperson. Try to protect yourself by including a hold-back clause in the contract.

INDEX